Crimes of hate, conspiracy of silence
Torture and ill-treatment based on sexual identity

This report is one of a series of publications issued by Amnesty International as part of its worldwide campaign against torture. Other reports issued as part of the campaign, which was launched in October 2000, include: ***Take a step to stamp out torture*** (AI Index: ACT 40/013/2000); ***Hidden scandal, secret shame — Torture and ill-treatment of children*** (AI Index: ACT 40/038/2000); ***Broken bodies, shattered minds — Torture and ill-treatment of women*** (AI Index: ACT 40/001/2001); and ***Stopping the torture trade*** (AI Index: ACT 40/002/2001). The campaign aims to galvanize people around the world to join the struggle to end torture.

- Take a step to stamp out torture — join Amnesty International's campaign against torture
- Join Amnesty International and other local and international human rights organizations which fight torture
- Make a donation to support Amnesty International's work
- Tell friends and family about the campaign and ask them to join too
- Register to take action against torture at *www.stoptorture.org* and campaign online. Visitors to the website will be able to appeal on behalf of individuals at risk of torture

Cover: Floral tributes near the Admiral Duncan pub, a gay bar in London, United Kingdom, where a nail-bomb explosion on 30 April 1999 killed three people and injured dozens of others. Gary Reid, a survivor of the blast, said, "The fear, loathing, hatred and ignorance culminating in these bombings is a warning to society and the world as a whole that racism, prejudice, homophobia and fear of difference is out there and we should all challenge it at every opportunity."
© Michael Crabtree/Reuters

Amnesty International (AI) is a worldwide movement of people who campaign for human rights. AI works towards the observance of all human rights as enshrined in the Universal Declaration of Human Rights and other international standards. It seeks to promote the observance of the full range of human rights, which it considers to be indivisible and interdependent, through campaigning and public awareness activities, as well as through human rights education and pushing for ratification and implementation of human rights treaties.

AI's work is based on careful research and on the standards agreed by the international community. AI is a voluntary, democratic, self-governing movement with more than a million members and supporters in more than 140 countries and territories. It is funded largely by its worldwide membership and by donations from the public. No funds are sought or accepted from governments for AI's work in documenting and campaigning against human rights violations.

AI is independent of any government, political persuasion or religious creed. It does not support or oppose any government or political system, nor does it support or oppose the views of the victims whose rights it seeks to protect. It is concerned solely with the impartial protection of human rights.

AI takes action against some of the gravest violations by governments of people's civil and political rights. The focus of its campaigning against human rights violations is to:

- free all prisoners of conscience. According to AI's statute, these are people detained for their political, religious or other conscientiously held beliefs or because of their ethnic origin, sex, colour, language, national or social origin, economic status, birth or other status – who have not used or advocated violence;
- ensure fair and prompt trials for all political prisoners;
- abolish the death penalty, torture and other ill-treatment of prisoners;
- end political killings and "disappearances".

AI calls on armed political groups to respect human rights and to halt abuses such as the detention of prisoners of conscience, hostage-taking, torture and unlawful killings.

AI also seeks to support the protection of human rights by other activities, including its work with the United Nations (UN) and regional intergovernmental organizations, and its work for refugees, on international military, security and police relations, and on economic and cultural relations.

Crimes of hate, conspiracy of silence
Torture and ill-treatment based on sexual identity

Amnesty International Publications

Please note that readers may find some of the photographs and case histories contained in this report disturbing.

First published in 2001 by
Amnesty International Publications
1 Easton Street
London WC1X oDW
United Kingdom

www.amnesty.org

© Copyright
Amnesty International Publications 2001
ISBN: 0 86210 302 9
AI Index: ACT 40/016/2001
Original language: English

Printed by:
The Alden Press
Osney Mead
Oxford
United Kingdom

CONTENTS

PREFACE   vii

INTRODUCTION   I
   Torture and sexual identity   3
   'Less than human'   4
   Discrimination and impunity   6
   'A planetary minority'   II

CHAPTER 1: CRIMINALIZING HOMOSEXUALITY —
A LICENCE TO TORTURE   12
   Romania: 'I was treated like the lowest of the low'   13
   The Caribbean: a colonial legacy of cruelty   15
   Malaysia: a stick with which to beat opponents   18
   Cruel judicial punishments   19

CHAPTER 2: TORTURE AND ILL-TREATMENT BY POLICE   21
   Policing the barrier between male and female   24
   Policing public space   28

CHAPTER 3: TORTURE AND ILL-TREATMENT IN PRISONS   30
   Who you are, not what you do — identity,
   discrimination and risk   31

CHAPTER 4: FORCED MEDICAL TREATMENT IN STATE
INSTITUTIONS   35

CHAPTER 5: 'THE SEVERITY SHOWS THE HATRED' —
HOMOPHOBIC VIOLENCE IN THE COMMUNITY   39
   State responsibility for violence in the community   39
   Lesbians at risk in the home and community   43
   Young people at risk   45
   Extending protection   46

CHAPTER 6: FLEEING TORTURE BASED ON SEXUAL
IDENTITY   49

CHAPTER 7: 'FIGHTING FOR OUR LIVES' – HUMAN RIGHTS
DEFENDERS   53
    LGBT rights defenders at risk   56

CHAPTER 8: RECOMMENDATIONS   59

APPENDIX: AI's 12-Point Program for the Prevention of
Torture by Agents of the State   66

ENDNOTES   70

PREFACE

"The manner in which discrimination is experienced on grounds of race or sex or religion or disability varies considerably — there is difference in difference. The commonality that unites them all is the injury to dignity imposed upon people as a consequence of their belonging to certain groups...

"In the case of gays, history and experience teach us that the scarring comes not from poverty or powerlessness, but from invisibility. It is the tainting of desire, it is the attribution of perversity and shame to spontaneous bodily affection, it is the prohibition of the expression of love, it is the denial of full moral citizenship in society because you are what you are, that impinges on the dignity and self-worth of a group."

Justice Albie Sachs, Constitutional Court of South Africa, 1998[1]

A note on terminology

In matters of sexuality, the terms people use and identify with can vary widely from culture to culture. In this report the terms "lesbian", "gay", "bisexual" and "transgender" (LGBT) are used because they are the English terms most commonly used in the international human rights discourse. However, this is in no way intended to ignore the diversity of other terms and identities, nor to deny the cultural connotations attached to these terms.

In the interests of readability and in order to respect the wealth of terms, a variety of forms are used in this report, largely interchangeably. So, for example, the term "lesbian and gay human rights" should be read as shorthand for the human rights of lesbian, gay, bisexual and transgender people.

- ● ***Sexual orientation*** refers to a person's sexual and emotional attraction to people of the same gender (homosexual orientation), another gender (heterosexual orientation) or both genders (bisexual orientation).
- ● ***Gender identity*** refers to a person's experience of self-expression in relation to social constructions of masculinity or femininity (gender). A person may have a male or female gender identity, with the physiological characteristics of the opposite sex.
- ● ***Sexual identity*** is used in this report to refer to sexual orientation and/or gender identity.
- ● ***Transgender*** identity refers to a compelling sense that one's gender identity is not in conformity with the physiological characteristics of the sex one is born with. This may lead some to seek "gender reassignment", usually involving hormones or surgery, to bring their physical characteristics into conformity with their gender identity.

Celebrate the Universal Declaration of Human Rights

Campaign for
DEMOCRACY
PEACE and
FREEDOM
in Africa

© Galz

Lesbian and Gay people in Africa
    demand EQUALITY and FREEDOM

INTRODUCTION

"Coming midnight, they said 'we want to show you something'. They took my clothes off and raped me. I remember being raped by two of them, then I passed out."[2]
Christine[3] was tortured in a secret detention centre in Uganda. She was raped after being left alone in a room with three male detainees. She was detained because she is a lesbian and in Uganda homosexuality is not just a social taboo, it is a criminal offence.

Christine and four of her friends — Paul, Norah, Rodney and Charles — formed a human rights group in early 1999. All five were gay and lesbian human rights defenders and so faced particular obstacles in Uganda where "carnal knowledge of any person against the order of nature", is an offence which can carry a sentence of life imprisonment.

In September 1999, in the wake of publicity in the Ugandan media about an alleged "gay marriage" in Kampala, President Yoweri Museveni announced to the press that he had ordered the Criminal Investigations Department "to look for homosexuals, lock them up and charge them".[4] The effect of this statement on the lives of the five activists was devastating.

Following the President's announcement, the five friends met at Christine's home in early October 1999 to discuss strategy. Somehow, the military found out about their meeting. At around 10pm, eight armed men burst into the room and arrested the five friends. Christine recalled, "No one could speak. We were all shocked... They tied black cloths on our heads and led us to the cars."

A poster produced by lesbian and gay rights organizations in southern Africa to mark the 50th anniversary in 1998 of the Universal Declaration of Human Rights, which proclaims that "All are equal before the law and are entitled without discrimination to equal protection of the law."

When they took the blindfold off, Christine found herself in a secret detention centre. She was stripped naked, beaten and threatened with rape by the soldiers holding her. She was then taken to another detention centre where she was interrogated about the human rights group the friends had set up and about her sexuality. "They asked me why I was not married. I told them I was not interested in marriage. They asked me if I knew homosexuality was taboo in Africa. I kept quiet.

1

They said it was a criminal offence and I could get a 10-year or life sentence. In the middle of that a policewoman came in and said 'I heard there was a lesbian here, can you do [to me] what you do to women?' I held my head high so she slapped me."

Rodney was taken to a military barracks. He recalled, "I was kicked in the chest four times. I was slapped. I was also shown electric cable that could be used on me if I did not tell them about our organisation..." He was held with a large number of military prisoners. "Learning that I was not a soldier and I was a gay activist they tortured me by kicking me on my stomach and slapping my face until I bled. I was made to sleep in a small toilet. The next day I was told to clean the toilet for one week, twice a day using my bare hands... I lost my trust in God. I came to believe that it is true that God hates those who are gay, as the local church claims and preaches."[5]

Norah was taken to another military barracks. "I was kept in a small filthy room with bats in the ceiling. I was by myself in that room for about five hours, then three men came in and started interrogating me. These men were so cruel and intimidating, it was unbearable... I was also beaten, abused both sexually and physically. My clothes were ripped off. Nasty remarks were made that I should just be punished for denying men what is rightfully theirs, and that who do I think I am to do what the president feels to be wrong. They even suggested that they should show me what I am missing by taking turns on me."[6]

Charles, the youngest of the five, was also interrogated at a military detention centre and threatened with death. He was held with five rebel suspects. "They said anyone who works against the government is a rebel."[7]

The five activists were released some two weeks later. Fearing for their safety if they returned to their homes, they fled to a neighbouring country. After days of travelling in harsh conditions, they arrived, tired and sick, in the capital. However, they were fearful of claiming asylum in a country which also criminalizes homosexuality and were forced to spend several months in hiding while they tried to find a way to get protection as refugees. All five required medical treatment following their ordeal. The psychological scars will take even longer to heal. Yet the experience has not daunted their determination to ensure that in future lesbian and gay Ugandans can live their lives in safety and dignity. Rodney summed up their courage and resolution:

"It will take me a long time to forget the torture I went through in Uganda and I hope that one day I shall return to Uganda and establish my LGBT centre without fear... I want to return to Africa to teach about human rights to promote the freedom of the LGBT persons. Maybe not today, not tomorrow, but soon."[8]

Torture and sexual identity

Torture and other cruel, inhuman or degrading treatment are prohibited under international human rights law. Yet in countries all over the world, lesbians, gay men and bisexual and transgender people are being tortured or ill-treated by state officials, or with their acquiescence, because of their sexual identity.

UN Convention against Torture

Article 1: "For the purposes of this Convention, the term "torture" means any act by which severe pain or suffering, whether physical or mental, is intentionally inflicted on a person for such purposes as obtaining from him or a third person information or a confession, punishing him for an act he or a third person has committed or is suspected of having committed, or intimidating or coercing him or a third person, or for any reason based on discrimination of any kind, when such pain or suffering is inflicted by or at the instigation of or with the consent or acquiescence of a public official or other person acting in an official capacity. It does not include pain or suffering arising only from, inherent in or incidental to lawful sanctions."

In the past AI's work against torture has highlighted the plight of those subjected to torture in a political context, such as opposition activists or journalists. Christine, Norah, Paul, Rodney and Charles are dissidents of a different kind, targeted not only because of their opinions or activism, but on account of their very identities. The victims of torture highlighted in this report include lesbian, gay, bisexual and transgender rights activists seen as threatening the social order; women seeking to exercise autonomy over their bodies; men seen as traitors to masculine privilege because they are perceived as adopting "feminine" roles; and transgender people calling into question the traditional assumption that all humankind must fall irrevocably into one of two gender categories. Defiance of the "heterosexual norm" can provoke moral condemnation, exclusion and violence, including torture. In this sense, violence against LGBT people is gender-based violence, inflicted on those who challenge or fail to conform to traditionally defined gender roles.

'Less than human'

In many parts of the world, being gay or lesbian is not seen as a right, but as a wrong. Homosexuality is considered a sin or an illness, a social or ideological deviation, or a betrayal of one's culture. Whereas most governments either deny practising human rights violations or portray them as rare aberrations, the repression that LGBT people face is often openly and passionately defended in the name of culture, religion, morality or public health, and facilitated by specific legal provisions.

In some countries, AIDS has been labelled a "gay plague", and homosexuality "the white man's disease". Same-sex relations are dubbed "unChristian", "unAfrican", "unIslamic" or a "bourgeois decadence". Some governments seek not only to exclude lesbian and gay people from local culture, but also to deny that they are members of the human race. For example, in 1995 President Robert Mugabe of Zimbabwe branded gays as "less than human". This dehumanization provides fertile ground for torture and ill-treatment. If LGBT people are "less than human", how can they have human rights? The denial of a person's basic humanity is the first step towards inhuman, cruel and degrading treatment.

History has shown how the language of dehumanization paves the way for atrocities against stigmatized groups in society. Differences of ethnicity, gender, religious affiliation and sexual orientation become boundaries drawn to exclude certain people from citizenship and even from membership of the human family. Like racism or sexism, homophobia is not "natural" or "inevitable". Discrimination based on identity can be manufactured, stoked or inflamed for political purposes. Governments in all continents have whipped up anti-gay sentiment and used it in a calculated and conscious way to attack their opponents, court support or deflect attention away from their own misdeeds and shortcomings. They have sought to use gay people as convenient scapegoats for perceived social ills, such as a break-down in morality or law and order.

In Namibia, for example, the Home Affairs Minister, Jerry Ekandjo, was reported on state television to have urged newly graduated police officers to "eliminate" gay men and lesbians "from the face of Namibia".[9] The recent spate of anti-gay pronouncements by certain African leaders has been seen by some local commentators as a tactic designed to deflect accusations of corruption and economic mismanagement.[10]

Inflammatory rhetoric by government leaders has also acted as an incitement to state officials to torture or ill-treat members of sexual minority groups with impunity. As this report illustrates, this can occur at the hands of the police, in prison or in other state institutions.

However, torture and ill-treatment by state officials is only the tip of the iceberg of violence targeted against LGBT people. For many, the most common experience of violence will be in their homes, schools and places of work or on the street. Torture is part of a broader spectrum of violence; while the perpetrators and settings may vary, what all forms of homophobic violence have in common is ignorance and prejudice within society that gives rise to such violence, official discrimination and repression that allows it, and the impunity that sustains it.

AI considers that acts of violence against lesbians, gay men and bisexual and transgender people in the home or the community constitute torture for which the state is accountable when they are of the nature and severity envisaged by the concept of torture in international standards and the state has failed to fulfil its obligation to provide effective protection.

Discrimination and impunity

Around the world, lesbians, gay men and bisexual and transgender people are imprisoned under laws which police the bedroom and criminalize a kiss; they are tortured to extract confessions of "deviance" and raped to "cure" them of it; they are killed by "death squads" in societies which view them as "*desechables*" – disposable garbage.

Lesbians, gay men and transgender and bisexual people may be targeted for persecution and violence for the same reason – because they are all considered "gender outlaws". But the ways and means in which that violence manifests itself can vary enormously. LGBT people's vulnerability to violence will also depend on such factors as gender, ethnicity and economic status. Such factors may also affect the victim's access to justice.

In virtually every part of the globe, LGBT lives are constrained by a web of laws and social practices which deny them an equal right to life, liberty and physical security, as well as other fundamental rights such as freedom of association, freedom of expression and rights to private life, employment, education and health care. While the degree to which discrimination is institutionalized varies from country to country, almost nowhere are LGBT people treated as fully equal before the law.

Abuses are often hidden behind a veil of silence and indifference. The taboo surrounding homosexuality means that most attacks on gay people are not reported. Fear of arrest and reprisals often prevents people from making complaints against the authorities. When lesbians and gays do report attacks in their homes and communities, the authorities frequently fail to take action on the grounds that these are "private" matters beyond their jurisdiction or an inevitable consequence of the victim's own actions. Official acquiescence allows violence against LGBT people to thrive.

This has been especially true of violence against women. Whereas male homosexuality is often proscribed in domestic law, in many countries it is assumed that women's sexuality needs no legal regulation. In many societies the sexuality of women, including lesbians, who choose to exercise autonomy over their own bodies, is controlled and suppressed through violence in the so-called "private" sphere of the home or the community. This may take the form of abuses such as rape or severe beatings which, if inflicted at the hands of state officials, would clearly be recognized as torture. The fact that such acts are perpetrated by private individuals rather than agents of the state does not absolve the authorities of their responsibility: the state may be held accountable under international human rights standards when these abuses persist owing to the complicity, acquiescence or lack of due diligence of the authorities.

Sexual orientation, like gender or race, relates to fundamental aspects of human identity. As the opening words of the Universal Declaration of Human Rights affirm, human rights are founded on the concept of respect for the inherent dignity and worth of the human person. Laws and practices aimed at coercing individuals to alter or deny their sexual orientation, or punishing them for not doing so, attack a deeply rooted aspect of human personality. They inflict huge psychological as well as physical violence because they force some people to forego an area of experience which, for many, offers the greatest potential for human fulfilment.

Because it relates to the deepest affairs of the heart, the innermost desires of the mind and the most intimate expressions of the body, sexual orientation goes to the core of a person's right to physical and mental integrity. That right must include the freedom to determine and express one's sexual orientation and to do so on the basis of equality — free of fear and discrimination.

The abuses against gay men and lesbians documented by AI violate some of the basic rights protected under international standards including the International Covenant on Civil and Political Rights (ICCPR) and the International Covenant on Economic, Social and Cultural Rights. Affirming lesbian and gay rights as human rights does not mean claiming new or "special" rights. It means demanding that everyone, regardless of sexual orientation, is guaranteed the fullest enjoyment of their civil, political, social, economic and cultural rights.

LGBT people have begun to use the mechanisms created under international and regional standards to assert this

International human rights standards on torture and ill-treatment

Torture is prohibited in numerous international standards. The prohibition is absolute and applies in all circumstances. There can be no justification, and states are obliged to prosecute those suspected of ordering or committing acts of torture.

1. Universal Declaration of Human Rights: "No one shall be subjected to torture or to cruel, inhuman or degrading treatment or punishment." (Article 5)
2. The UN Convention against Torture and Other Cruel, Inhuman or Degrading Treatment or Punishment (Convention against Torture) prohibits torture carried out "by or at the instigation of or with the consent or acquiescence of a public official or other person acting in an official capacity". (Article 1)
3. The International Covenant on Civil and Political Rights (ICCPR) also prohibits torture and ill-treatment even "in times of emergency threatening the life of the nation". The UN Human Rights Committee, an expert body that monitors states' compliance with the ICCPR, has stated: "it is the duty of the State Party to afford everyone protection through legislative and other measures as may be necessary against acts prohibited in Article 7 [prohibiting torture and ill-treatment], whether inflicted by people acting in their official capacity, outside of their official capacity or in a private capacity..."[11]

Torture and ill-treatment are also prohibited under regional human rights instruments — such as the Inter-American Convention to Prevent and Punish Torture, and the European Convention for the Protection of Human Rights and Fundamental Freedoms (European Convention on Human Rights), as well as standards relating to specific groups such as the UN Convention on the Rights of the Child and the International Convention on the Elimination of All Forms of Racial Discrimination.

International law prohibits not only torture, but also acts which do not amount to torture, but nevertheless constitute "cruel, inhuman or degrading treatment or punishment" (ill-treatment). This prohibition is also absolute and applies in all circumstances.[12] The scope of the terms was clearly meant to be broad, and interpreted so as to extend the widest possible protection against physical or mental abuse.[13]

demand. Since the 1980s, three separate complaints by gay men from Northern Ireland, the Republic of Ireland and Cyprus have led to rulings by the European Court of Human Rights that laws criminalizing same-sex relations between adult men are in breach of the right to privacy protected in the European Convention on Human Rights.[14]

© Gay Times

Nick Toonen (left) and Rodney Croome

In 1992, Nick Toonen brought a complaint against a similar law in the Australian state of Tasmania before the UN Human Rights Committee, which monitors states' compliance with the ICCPR. In 1994, the Committee found that the law violated the right to privacy jointly with the right to freedom from discrimination. The Committee noted that reference to "sex" in the non-discrimination clauses of the ICCPR — Articles 2(1) and 26 — should be taken as including "sexual orientation", thereby affirming that the rights set out in the ICCPR cannot be denied to any individual because of their sexual orientation.[15] Other UN human rights monitoring bodies have also emphasized that discrimination on the basis of sexual orientation is prohibited under international legal standards.[16]

In addition, the European Court of Human Rights has ruled that prohibiting a transsexual from adopting a feminine name or changing her civil status was contrary to Article 8 of the European Convention on Human Rights, which deals with the right to privacy,[17] and the European Court of Justice has ruled that a transsexual teacher, sacked after undergoing gender reassignment surgery, was unfairly dismissed, on grounds of discrimination.[18]

The UN Human Rights Committee has since urged states not only to repeal laws criminalizing homosexuality but also to enshrine the prohibition of discrimination based on sexual orientation into their constitutions or other fundamental laws.[19]

Women's sexual rights were also advanced at the UN World Conference on women in 1995, which adopted the Beijing Platform for Action. Paragraph 96 of the Platform for Action states: "The human rights of women include their right to have control over and decide freely and responsibly on matters related to their sexuality, including sexual and reproductive health, free of coercion, discrimination and violence."

Lesbian participants in the first gay and lesbian parade held in the Philippines, June 1996.

© Reuters

'A planetary minority'

A vocal and vibrant movement has now emerged around the world to break the conspiracy of silence surrounding discrimination and violence against LGBT people. It is challenging the rhetoric of governments who seek to deny that same-sex sexual identity or behaviour exist in all cultures. In the words of Indian gay rights activist Ashok Row Kavi, "we are truly international and we are truly a planetary minority". While this global activism has diverse roots, it has grown in part out of the movement for women's rights — including women's sexual rights.

By campaigning for an end to torture and ill-treatment against LGBT people, AI seeks to promote the fundamental principle of universality. If we tolerate the denial of rights to any group, we undermine the whole protective framework of human rights by taking away its central plank — the equal rights and dignity of all human beings. The right not to be subjected to torture and ill-treatment must apply to every human being without distinction.

This report focuses primarily on torture and ill-treatment by state officials, the core of AI's research in recent years. However, it also explores the responsibility of states to prevent and punish violence in the broader community. It is important to recognize that the different patterns of violence against LGBT people — whether in police custody, in prison, in the community or in the home — form a continuum. Addressing this spectrum of violence within the framework of torture and ill-treatment highlights the gravity of these abuses, wherever they occur. It also underscores the obligations of states to address both the violence and the discrimination that gives rise to it.

This report is not an exhaustive global survey of torture and ill-treatment of LGBT people based on sexual identity. The cases featured are intended as illustrative of the patterns of violence which AI has documented in many countries. It is intended to inform and support the work of AI members and other activists around the world who are campaigning to raise awareness about the torture and ill-treatment of lesbians, gay men, and bisexual and transgender people and pressing for concrete measures to support those at risk and to prevent these abuses.

11

1: CRIMINALIZING HOMOSEXUALITY — A LICENCE TO TORTURE

In 1592, a woman named Felipa de Souza living in the Portuguese colony of Brazil was sentenced by the Roman Catholic Inquisition for the "nefarious and abominable crime of sodomy" after admitting that she had had sexual relations with other women. She was condemned to exile and was viciously whipped while walking the streets of Salvador to serve as an example to others.[20]

The criminalization of homosexuality and the infliction of torture as a penalty for the crime may sound medieval, but Felipa has many modern counterparts. At least 70 states have entered the 21st century with laws on their statute books prohibiting same-sex relations.[21] In some countries same-sex relations can incur the death penalty. Many of the reports AI has received of torture or ill-treatment of LGBT people in detention have come from countries where same-sex relations are outlawed.

In every society, the criminal law regulates the boundaries of permissible sexual behaviour, placing such constraints on individual sexual expression and fulfilment as are necessary to safeguard the rights of others. Such boundaries vary across cultures and shift throughout history as archaic proscriptions are lifted and new rights recognized. The elastic term "sodomy" has often been used by legislators to describe what lies beyond those boundaries. Among the many "deviant" practices which in the past have been brought within its scope in different countries are inter-racial sexual relations and any sexual act not leading to procreation.

Laws criminalizing homosexual relations exist on all continents, albeit in different forms.[22] In some countries, consensual sex between adults of the same sex is criminalized as "sodomy", "crimes against nature" or "unnatural acts". In others, vague provisions such as "immoral acts" or "public scandal" are used to criminalize different expressions of homosexual identity. In many parts of the world, such laws are the remnants of colonial domination, although ironically they are defended by some post-colonial government leaders as a necessary safeguard against what they describe as the "foreign import" of homosexuality. AI opposes all laws allowing for the imprisonment of people solely for their sexual identity. People detained or imprisoned under such laws are considered prisoners of conscience and should be released immediately and unconditionally.

AI's research indicates that such laws can also act as a licence to torture and ill-treat in a number of ways. For example, in some countries, corporal punishments such as flogging are imposed judicially — that is, by a court of law — for the "crime" of homosexuality. AI considers that such punishments constitute torture or other cruel, inhuman or degrading punishment.

Laws criminalizing homosexuality may also encourage law enforcement officials to disregard the humanity of the detainee whose very identity is criminalized. By institutionalizing discrimination, they can act as an official incitement to violence against LGBT people in the community as a whole, whether in custody, in prison, on the street or in the home. By stripping a sector of the population of their full rights, they also deprive lesbian and gay victims of torture or ill-treatment of access to redress and allow their torturers to continue abusing others with impunity.

Romania: 'I was treated like the lowest of the low'

Mariana Cetiner[23] was arrested in October 1995 for "attempting to seduce another woman". In June 1996, she was convicted and sentenced under Article 200 of the Romanian Penal Code to three years' imprisonment. "I was treated very badly by the prison guards, because in Romania there is no approval for those who have had relations between the same sex. And worse, the guards... beat me and insulted me. Criminals are better regarded than a relationship between two women... So because of this homosexual or lesbian thing... I was treated like the lowest of the low."[24]

In one incident in August 1996, when Mariana Cetiner complained about her ill-treatment, she was handcuffed to a

radiator and made to stand for 11 hours "in a position like Jesus Christ" without food. Although acquitted on appeal in January 1997, she was later rearrested when a court of third instance reversed this decision and she was ordered to serve the remainder of the sentence. Mariana Cetiner was taken to another penitentiary where she was placed in a high security cell for violent detainees and was beaten both by

Mariana Cetiner was beaten and tortured by prison guards in Romania after being arrested in 1995, and then sentenced to three years' imprisonment in 1996 for "attempting to seduce another woman".

guards and other inmates. She said that in one incident she was left with broken ribs. When she asked to see a doctor she was placed in solitary confinement for 10 days.

Following international pressure, including a sustained campaign of demonstrations and letter-writing by AI members around the world, Mariana Cetiner was released by presidential decree in March 1998. She left Romania shortly afterwards.

The criminalization of homosexuality in Romania has for many years created a fertile environment for torture. Article 200 of the Penal Code was revised in 1996, under pressure from the Council of Europe. However, it continues to provide for imprisonment for private consensual homosexual relations where these are deemed to cause "public scandal".[25] Article 200, paragraph 5, makes it an offence, punishable by a sentence of between one and five years' imprisonment, "to entice or seduce a person to practise same-sex acts, as well as to engage in other forms of proselytizing with the same aim." Reforms to the Penal Code proposed by the government in September 1999, including abolition of Article 200, had not been adopted by parliament by early 2001.

In September 1996, two 17-year-old boys were arrested in a park at night, charged under the new provision, and severely beaten by police to force them to confess to having sex in public. "They wanted to know who else I did it with and they beat me sadistically to get names and addresses... They were always asking who was the girl, who was the boy. I would tell them, 'We are both boys': then they'd slap and hit me. We were like two punching bags."[26]

No investigation is known to have taken place into these reports of torture or ill-treatment.

The Caribbean: a colonial legacy of cruelty

Although laws proscribing homosexual relations are defended in the name of local cultural values, such laws in many Caribbean countries are a legacy of the colonial past. The passionate defence of "sodomy" laws by certain Caribbean governments perpetuates discrimination and creates a climate conducive to violence against lesbian and gay people, both at the hands of state officials and of others in the community. In a submission to the UN Human Rights Committee on Trinidad and Tobago in October 2000, AI stated that the retention of laws which treat homosexuals as criminals lends support to a climate of prejudice which increases the risk of attacks and other abuses against people believed to be gay or lesbian. Reports suggest that such laws are often used by the police to extort money from members of the gay community.

Four men were arrested near the airport in Kingston, Jamaica, in November 1996 and charged with "gross indecency". The men, two of whom were partially clothed, were forced to remove all their clothes and held naked in public view at the

© Eric Miller/Panos

airport police post until the following day. An angry mob gathered, allegedly in response to incitement by police officers, and threatened the men. The four were then driven to the Rape Unit where they were allegedly sexually assaulted before being transferred to the Remand Centre where they were forced to clean other inmates' cells and toilets with their bare hands. Police also incited other inmates to assault the men and left their cells unlocked so that other inmates could enter and beat them.

A lesbian, gay, bisexual and transgender rights march in Cape Town, South Africa, in 1993. In 1998 the South African Constitutional Court ruled that laws criminalizing sodomy (referring to consensual sex between men) violated the rights to equality, dignity and privacy enshrined in the post-apartheid Constitution.

This is one of a large number of reports received by AI of ill-treatment of gay people in Jamaica. Most reports are anecdotal or anonymous, usually because individuals fear reprisals if they complain. Consensual sex between men remains punishable by up to 10 years' imprisonment with hard labour.[27] Such laws appear to be seen by law enforcement officials as a licence to ill-treat people believed to be homosexual. They also encourage physical attacks against gay people in the broader community.

Cases of homophobic ill-treatment have also been reported in Caribbean countries where same-sex relations in private have been decriminalized. In the Bahamas, two 17-year-old youths

© ACLU

The Reverend Margarita Sanchez (left) and attorney Nora Vargas (right) have challenged the law in Puerto Rico, USA, under which anyone who "has sexual intercourse with people of the same sex or commits the crime against nature with a human being" may face 10 years' imprisonment.

were arrested by police in August 1999 on suspicion of having sex in a car parked on a secluded beach in Nassau. They were forced to strip and were beaten with an iron bar. At the police station they were subjected to homophobic insults and refused permission to put on their undergarments or to contact relatives or lawyers. In January 2000 the government said that the incident was being investigated. In February 2001 the Acting Commissioner of Police Management Services wrote to AI stating that "an investigation was conducted and I am satisfied that there was no CIDT [cruel, inhuman or degrading treatment] meted out to anyone in custody." The letter did not respond to AI's detailed concerns or give any information about the scope or conduct of the investigation.

Some Caribbean governments defend "sodomy" laws as necessary for the prevention of HIV/AIDS. The exclusive linkage of HIV/AIDS to homosexuality is not only discriminatory, but factually inaccurate and dangerous. The UN Human Rights Committee has noted that laws criminalizing "unnatural sexual intercourse" are an obstacle to HIV prevention work.[28] Such laws can result in AIDS awareness workers being detained and ill-treated on suspicion of promoting homosexual relations. On 5 May 2000 a nurse was detained while distributing condoms to sex workers in Jamaica, despite carrying identification authorizing him to carry out his work. He was held by police for nine hours, denied access to his family or to a lawyer, interrogated and verbally abused before being released without charge. The criminalization of same-sex relations in Jamaica is also a formidable barrier to safe sex initiatives in prisons, leaving detainees highly vulnerable to infection (see Chapter 3: Torture and ill-treatment in prisons).

Malaysia: a stick with which to beat opponents

Governments around the world have used homophobia as a convenient tool for diverting public attention or discrediting and silencing their opponents. Accusations of homosexuality have been used as a pretext to imprison political opponents, and torture and ill-treatment have been used to extract confessions in order to make fabricated charges stick.

In Malaysia, "carnal intercourse against the order of nature" is punishable by up to 20 years' imprisonment and whipping.[29] In early September 1998, former Deputy Prime Minister Anwar Ibrahim was dismissed by Prime Minister Mahathir Mohamad amid accusations of sexual misconduct, corruption and threatening national security. AI believes the accusations were a politically motivated response to Anwar Ibrahim's calls for political reform. Three weeks later, immediately after Anwar Ibrahim had been arrested and held incommunicado in police detention and severely beaten, Prime Minister Mahathir publicly branded him a "sodomist, unfit to rule the country".

Before Anwar Ibrahim's arrest, two men — Munawar Anees, his former speech writer, and Sukma Darmawan, Anwar Ibrahim's adopted brother — were sentenced to six months' imprisonment for "outrages on decency". They had been forced under torture to confess to having "allowed themselves to be sodomized" by Anwar Ibrahim. They were forced to undergo various forms of humiliating and sexual ill-treatment, such as being stripped naked and forced to simulate the sexual acts they were accused of. Another man, Mior Abdul Razak, was also accused of similar sexual offences involving Anwar Ibrahim. The three men lodged formal complaints against the police about their treatment and coerced confessions. Sukma Darmawan and Mior Abdul Razak were charged with perjury; Munawar Anees was allowed to leave the country.

In 1999, Anwar Ibrahim and Sukma Darmawan went on trial on charges of "sodomy". Sukma Darmawan's confession was admitted as evidence, despite his testimony that it had been extracted under torture. In August 2000, both men were found guilty; Anwar Ibrahim was sentenced to nine years in prison, and Sukma Darmawan was sentenced to six years' imprisonment and four strokes of the cane. At the time of writing, appeals by both men were pending. Sukma Darmawan remained free on bail pending the result of his appeal. Anwar Ibrahim was serving his prison sentence and was a prisoner of conscience.

Following widespread protests, a former national police chief was sentenced in March 2000 to two months in prison for beating Anwar Ibrahim. To AI's knowledge, no one has been brought to justice for the torture of Sukma Darmawan and Munawar Anees. The relevant sections of the Penal Code remain in force.[30]

Cruel judicial punishments

Malaysia is not the only country where corporal punishment can be applied by law as a sanction for same-sex relations. On 16 April 2000, *Associated Press* reported that a Saudi Arabian court had sentenced nine young men to prison sentences and up to 2,600 lashes each for "deviant sexual behaviour", apparently because of their sexual identity.[31]

The imposition of such penalties for same-sex sexual relations must be viewed in the context of the repression of other forms of consensual sexual behaviour which are seen to transgress strict religious or political codes, such as sexual relations between men and women outside marriage. Where gender discrimination is enshrined in law, women accused of any kind of sexual activity outside marriage are particularly at risk of such penalties.[32]

Under some interpretations of Islamic (*Shari'a*) law, punishment for sexual relations outside marriage, including same-sex sexual behaviour, can entail up to 100 lashes for unmarried people and stoning to death for married people. In Afghanistan at least six men were reported to have been publicly crushed to death in two separate cases in 1998 and 1999 after being convicted of "sodomy" by a *Taleban* court.[33] In Chechnya, the *Shari'a* Criminal Code provides for the death penalty for male homosexual acts. AI opposes the death penalty in all cases as the ultimate cruel, inhuman and degrading punishment.

Gay and lesbian members of AI and others at the 2001 Sydney Gay and Lesbian Mardi Gras in Australia.

© Craig Cranko

2: TORTURE AND ILL-TREATMENT BY POLICE

© Windy City Times/www.wctimes.com

Frederick Mason reported being tortured by police in Chicago, USA, in July 2000. Racism and homophobia appear to have played a central role in the attack on him.

Frederick Mason, a 31-year-old nurse's assistant, was arrested in Chicago, USA, in July 2000 after an argument with his landlord. According to witnesses, Frederick Mason entered the police station in good health. However, by the time he was released blood was streaming from his rectum. According to his testimony, two unidentified police officers took him to the interrogation room where he was handcuffed by the elbows, and pinned to a wall. The arresting officer then reportedly pulled down Frederick Mason's pants and sprayed blue cleaning liquid on a billy club before ramming the baton into his rectum. As he sodomized Frederick Mason, the officer is alleged have hurled homophobic insults at him. A second unidentified officer is alleged to have witnessed Frederick Mason's pants being pulled down, but walked away during the assault. Frederick Mason contends that he was subjected to abuse — including racist and anti-gay insults such as "nigger fag"— from the moment he was arrested.

On 25 November 2000, Jeffrey Lyons, a 39-year-old heterosexual man, was allegedly assaulted by a group of between eight and 10 off-duty Chicago police officers after they witnessed him embracing a male friend outside a bar. The assault left him with severe injuries including a broken nose, fractured cheekbone and neurological damage. Towards the end of the assault an unidentified officer reportedly taunted him by saying "Get this through your head, you faggots will never win". After Jeffrey Lyons briefly lost consciousness the officers dispersed and the main perpetrator returned to the bar.

According to reports, two of the cars that fled the scene — later traced to off-duty police officers' vehicles — attempted to run over Jeffrey Lyons' companion as he took notes of their licence plate numbers.

Both cases were under investigation by the police department's Office of Professional Standards, the police complaints authority, at the time of writing. However, local sources have expressed concern that the investigation may be hampered by officers' attempts to cover up the incidents. Three officers implicated in the assault on Jeffrey Lyons were initially suspended but have since returned to duty.

In the USA, New York police officers beat peaceful demonstrators attending a rally organized by lesbian and gay rights activists. The rally was protesting against the murder of Matthew Shepard, a student battered to death in Wyoming, USA, in October 1998. In January 2001 the courts awarded damages to three demonstrators who were injured by police horses.

AI called on the Chicago city and police authorities to ensure that a thorough and impartial investigation was conducted to send a clear signal that torture and ill-treatment by police officers, including homophobic abuse, will not be tolerated.34

Even when the law does not penalize gay identity or behaviour, the actions of police officers often do. Prejudice — whether in the form of racism, sexism or homophobia — means that certain people are particularly vulnerable to discrimination and ill-treatment in custody. Discrimination can also reinforce impunity for police officers responsible for torture or ill-treatment. When the victim belongs, or is perceived to belong, to a marginalized social group, officers are often able to act secure in the knowledge that their behaviour will not be investigated thoroughly, or indeed at all. In many instances the code of silence which deters officers from reporting abuses that take place within their ranks serves to protect those responsible for torture or ill-treatment. One of the consequences of this climate of impunity is that people whose rights have been violated are silenced, either because they do not feel able to report the abuse or because the police choose not to hear complaints.

Lesbian and gay prisoners are at heightened risk of sexual violence in custody. Many are subjected to persistent sexual harassment. Some are the victims of sexual assault, including rape. The failure of the authorities to tackle issues such as sexism and homophobia in police forces creates a climate in which such violations can easily proliferate.

In 1997, Katya Ivanova,[35] a lesbian living in Moscow in the Russian Federation, went to the local police station to lodge a complaint against neighbours who had assaulted and threatened her. She showed the officer dealing with her complaint the notes her neighbours had pushed under her door containing threats and homophobic abuse. As soon as he saw these, the officer began to sexually harass her. Katya Ivanova left the police station regretting that she had turned to the police for help. Several months later the officer summoned her to come to his office. Katya Ivanova assumed that he wished to see her in connection with her complaint; she was wrong. "He threatened that my neighbours might kill me, but that he would be able to help me. Then he told me that the only way he would help me is if I slept with him. When I attempted to resist him, he grabbed me and threw me on the table. He beat me in the face and raped me, right there in his office." In the next few months she was summoned on a number of occasions by the same officer to come to his office or to other locations. Knowing that if she did not respond she would be arrested and detained, Katya Ivanova met him. "Ostensibly, this was to investigate my case, but in reality, he called me in so that he could rape me again." Katya

Ivanova is now seeking asylum in the USA. "I pray that I am granted asylum so that my nightmare can finally end."[36]

Gay people arrested for reasons in no way connected with their sexuality can find that their sexual orientation is exploited by police during interrogation. In addition, interrogators may see sexual "dissidence" as linked to dissidence in other areas.

Bojan Aleksov, a gay man from the Federal Republic of Yugoslavia, was taken into police custody on 7 July 2000 by members of the State Security Service and questioned about his involvement with a Belgrade-based women's anti-war organization, Women in Black, and a project based in Budapest that defends the rights of conscientious objectors from the Federal Republic of Yugoslavia. The interrogators told Bojan Aleksov that they knew about his "support for deserters" and that those who associated with particular activists from Bosnia-Herzegovina "were idiots and enemies of our own country." "They said that I was being paid with foreign funds, and that the grant [for humanitarian work from a foundation in the West] was just a cover for intelligence and anti-state activities."

Bojan Aleksov says he was severely beaten during the interrogation, which lasted for almost 24 hours. He was told that police would fabricate a story about his death. "They continually yelled and swore at me, calling me various insulting names, most often 'peder' [queer]. At one point one of the interrogators took out a large car key and dangled it in front of my eyes and said that it would be a good fit (up my arse)."[37]

Bojan Aleksov was released after he was coerced into signing a statement that said that he and a Women in Black activist had been involved in intelligence activities and had been working to undermine the defence capabilities of Yugoslavia. He was also coerced into agreeing to work for the State Security service as an informer, but fled the country immediately, fearing what else might happen to him.

Policing the barrier between male and female

Vanessa Lorena Ledesma, a transgender woman, was arrested in Córdoba, Argentina, on 11 February 2000 during a scuffle at a

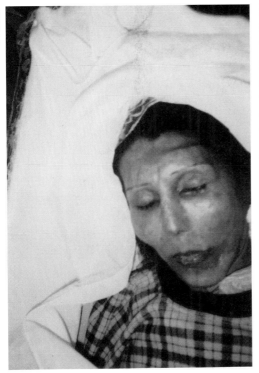

© Private

Vanessa Lorena Ledesma

bar. Five days later she was dead. A police report recorded that she had died as a result of a "cardiac arrest". However, an autopsy reportedly revealed that her body showed signs of torture, including severe bruising. At the police station she had reportedly been held incommunicado and segregated from other detainees, not for her own protection but so that other prisoners would not have to share a cell with "a sick person" — an allusion to her HIV-positive status. Following a demonstration in Buenos Aires by LGBT rights activists, the provincial authorities in Córdoba indicated that they would reopen investigations into Vanessa Lorena Ledesma's death.[38]

In many countries, transgender people face extremely high levels of discrimination and abuse. They are often treated as the ultimate "gender outlaws", punished not only for transgressing the socially constructed barriers of gender but, in some cases, for changing their biologically determined sex. For many, the "penalty" is violence, including torture.

In recent years, AI has documented alarming levels of abuses, including torture and ill-treatment, against transgender people in the Americas. The wealth of information about such attacks is in large part the result of the courageous work of local transgender rights activists who have battled against threats and marginalization to draw attention to these patterns of abuse.

In some countries in the region, transgender people may come into contact with the law simply for being who they are. In certain provinces in Argentina, for example, by-laws allow the police to detain people for vaguely defined offences against public decency, including cross-dressing. However, it is those involved in sex work who bear the brunt of police brutality across the region.

Extortion is a common underlying motive for the torture and ill-treatment of transgender sex workers. Three transvestites were arrested by Civil Police in Maceio, Brazil, in June 1997, allegedly for failing to pay an extortion "fee" to the police. At the police station they were brutally beaten with rubber sandals studded with nails and forced to clean filthy lavatories. On release, two of them, known as Aleska and Fabiana, fled to a "safe house", too terrified to make an official complaint.39

Aleska (left) and Fabiana, July 1997, Brazil.

© AI

Police ill-treatment has also occurred in the context of "social cleansing" operations targeting transgender sex workers who are blamed for the spread of disease. Nine transvestite sex workers were detained in Guayaquil, Ecuador, in July 2000 apparently on suspicion of being HIV-positive.40 Accused of "crimes against public morals", they were forced to undergo HIV tests. Local press reports talked of "AIDS-carriers" and "gays with AIDS on the loose".41 International standards on health and human rights prohibit forced testing in such circumstances,42 and AI believes that such aggressive testing amounts to cruel, inhuman and degrading treatment.

In Venezuela, two young transgender friends were detained by police in Valencia, Carabobo state, in August 2000. They were forced to undress in the street and severely beaten. The Carabobo police are also reported to have forced transgender people to perform sexual acts in return for release and to have dumped them semi-naked at some distance from the city if they refused.[43]

Transgender people are often attacked in other ways that strike at key physical manifestations of their transgender identity. For example, in numerous cases, male to female transsexuals or transvestites have been beaten on their cheekbones or breasts so as to burst their implants, sometimes causing the release of toxic substances with severe health consequences.

Transgender rights activists who have attempted to hold the police accountable for torture and ill-treatment have themselves faced physical violence. Nadia Echazu was detained and ill-treated by police in Buenos Aires, Argentina, in December 1997, the day she was due to give testimony to a tribunal investigating ill-treatment of transvestites at two police stations. She was taken to one of the police stations under investigation, where she was kicked, beaten and placed in a straitjacket, before being released without charge.[44]

More recently, Argentine LGBT activists campaigning for justice in the case of Vanessa Ledesma have also been targeted. Vanessa Piedrabuena, president of the United Córdoba Transvestites Association, signed the official complaint about Vanessa Ledesma's death. She was subsequently threatened and harassed at her home by police, who reportedly told her: "Keep your head down... Mind your own business. No one is going to look out for you when something happens to you."[45]

Following intense domestic and international pressure, a number of police officers were charged with the ill-treatment of Vanessa Ledesma. However, none was arrested or suspended and in mid-2000 proceedings against the police officers were halted.

Threats to and ill-treatment of activists may have been instrumental in ensuring police impunity, but they have not deterred LGBT people from the struggle.

© Ignacio Saiz

Lohana Berkins,
transgender rights
activist, Argentina.

"For years we have been working on building [our] right to full citizenship. We want the state to respect our right to an identity; we don't want to be marginalised from our homes and our schools, or to be condemned to prostitution, where we are subjected to the worst abuses. Many of our compañeras have been beaten to death in police stations and no one cries out or defends them."[46]

Lohana Berkins, Argentine
transgender rights activist

Policing public space

Police ill-treatment is not confined to the interrogation room or police station. Ill-treatment can also take place during raids on public meeting places or during demonstrations. In some countries around the world it is used to deny LGBT people access to public space and to prevent them from exercising their right to freedom of association and peaceful assembly.

In Ecuador, ill-treatment has been used as a method of preventing LGBT people from organizing and denying their presence in society. For example, police reportedly used tear gas against 300 people who had gathered peacefully in the centre of Guayaquil for a cultural parade organized by the *Fundación Amigos por la Vida*, Friends for Life Foundation, to mark Stonewall Day on 28 June 2000.[47] *Fundación Amigos por la Vida* had repeatedly sought authorization for the parade from the police authorities. This had been denied, reportedly on the grounds that society was not ready for such an event.

Police in Guayaquil have also clamped down on bars and other venues frequented by the local LGBT community. Tomás[48] was at a nightclub in the city when at around 3am the local police sub-lieutenant burst in. "I asked him very politely, 'What's happening, officer?' and that was enough for him to attack me, pushing me so that I fell down the stairs. He carried on beating me and insulting me for being gay."[49]

Tomás and a nightclub employee were taken away in a van. A few blocks away the van stopped and both men were forced to lie face down in the vehicle. Tomás was kicked and beaten until his face bled. At the police headquarters he was told to stand with his legs apart and hit several times with a broomstick. Another police officer involved in the arrest reportedly threatened to kill him if he reported the beating. There appears to have been no legitimate motive for the raid on the nightclub, whose licence was withdrawn. The two detainees were released without charge after two days.[50]

Police sweeps on lesbian bars have also been reported in recent years in Lima, Peru. In some cases these have resulted in beatings and homophobic verbal abuse. In the past, press crews have accompanied police during raids; for many LGBT people, the consequences of having their identity broadcast on television can be devastating.

In July 1997, armed police officers in Moscow, Russian Federation, allegedly beat and otherwise ill-treated several people during a raid on Chance, a lesbian and gay nightclub. Some 40 people were reportedly beaten during arrest and forced to sign pre-prepared statements containing falsified drug test results. AI's calls for an investigation into the allegations appear to have gone unheeded.

In India, the People's Union for Civil Liberties-Karnataka (PUCL-K) has documented a widespread pattern of police ill-treatment and extortion against gay and bisexual men in parks and other meeting places in Bangalore. For example, PUCL-K reported that 10 men were detained on 22 April 2000. Some were severely beaten. All were verbally abused and threatened that their families would be informed about their sexual orientation and arrest. PUCL-K noted that parks and other public areas are often the only spaces where gay people can meet and socialize, while women's access to public space is even more restricted. Lack of privacy in these areas leaves people vulnerable to anti-gay attacks by individuals who feel they can act with impunity; fear that their sexual identity will become known to families, colleagues or neighbours discourages most victims from lodging complaints.[51]

3: TORTURE AND ILL-TREATMENT IN PRISONS

"After I was raped they asked me if I had learned my lesson... [Guards] said that since I'm gay I ought to have enjoyed it."

Timothy Tucker, a gay HIV-positive man raped by another inmate in a federal prison in Virginia, USA.[52]

LGBT prisoners, and others perceived to be gay, are often at risk of torture and ill-treatment. Too often, they have little access to methods of seeking redress and are forced to endure in silence violence, sexual assault, coercion, humiliation, denial of medical treatment and other forms of ill-treatment.

On 7 December 2000, Luciano Rodríguez Linares, a gay prisoner at Topo Chico prison, Nuevo León State, Mexico, was taken out of his cell and beaten. Several prison officers held him down as another reportedly inserted a finger into his anus, drawing blood. Although ostensibly searching for drugs, the officer is reported to have said "If that's what you want, I'll give it to you", as other officers looked on and laughed. The officer told him he would be killed if he filed a complaint. In January 2001, AI again expressed concern to the authorities that Luciano Rodríguez was at risk of reprisals for having lodged the complaint.[53]

LGBT prisoners are at risk of violence from other inmates as well as prison officials. When the prison authorities, as agents of the state, fail to protect inmates from violence at the hands of other prisoners, they can be held accountable for torture or ill-treatment.

In Jamaica, where same-sex relations are illegal, 16 prisoners were killed and 40 injured in anti-gay attacks at St Catherine's District Prison and Kingston's General Penitentiary in August 1997. The disturbances started after the Commissioner of Corrections announced his intention to distribute condoms to guards and prisoners in an effort to control the spread of HIV/AIDS. Guards walked out in protest at the insinuation that they were having sexual relations with inmates. In the absence of supervision, inmates went on the rampage, targeting prisoners known or believed to be gay. No action is known to have been taken against those responsible for the violence.[54]

Despite the severity of such abuses, many prisoners fear seeking redress. LGBT prisoners may fear retaliation, breaches of confidentiality or not having their claims taken seriously by the authorities. As a spokesperson for a US non-governmental organization has commented, "Very few [abuses] are reported because of the tremendous stigma involved and because the life expectancy of a 'snitch' [someone who informs on others] behind bars is measured in minutes rather than days."[55] As a result assaults against LGBT prisoners, whether by guards or other inmates, are rarely investigated and even more rarely punished.

Prison guards have been implicated in actively promoting or fostering violence between inmates and allowing attacks on gay prisoners as a way of regulating the prison environment. "They would rather have prisoners doing violence to each other than to them. They use it as a management tool."[56] Kevin Mahoney, a gay man, died in the Corcoran Security Housing Unit in California, USA, in 1999. He had been left alone in the exercise yard with another inmate known to be dangerous; the inmate strangled him. The guards failed to intervene for between one and two hours, even though the murder was said to have been captured on camera.[57]

Gary Adkins, an inmate at Wayne County jail in West Virginia, USA, was believed to have been targeted for torture and ill-treatment because of his homosexuality. In October 1999 correctional officers sprayed mace in Gary Adkins' eyes for no apparent reason, beat him and then denied him medical treatment. Gary Adkins sustained broken ribs, a broken nose, contusions to the head and cuts and bruises as a result of the beating. The Federal Bureau of Investigation (FBI) launched an investigation; at the time of writing the FBI's report was under review by the US Department of Justice.[58]

Who you are, not what you do — identity, discrimination and risk

Prison authorities have an obligation to take effective measures to prevent violence against all prisoners including lesbian and gay prisoners. For female prisoners this means that they must be held separately from male prisoners and that they should not be supervised by male members of staff. Many women in prison face pervasive sexual harassment and assault. Lesbians and other women who are seen to transgress gender boundaries are often at heightened risk of torture and ill-treatment. Perceived or actual sexual orientation has been found to be one of four categories that make a female prisoner a more likely target for sexual abuse.[59]

© AI

Robin Lucas

Robin Lucas, an African-American woman, was incarcerated for credit card fraud in California, USA, in 1995. She was placed in the Special Housing Unit of the Federal Detention Center, Pleasanton. The prison authorities ignored her complaints about being in a unit generally housing men and about the fact that she was visible to male inmates and guards 24 hours a day, including when she showered and used the toilet. Robin Lucas also complained that she was harassed, taunted and threatened because of her sexual orientation. One evening in September 1995, three male inmates unlocked the door of her cell, handcuffed her and raped her. Robin Lucas suffered severe injuries to her neck, arms, back and vaginal and anal areas. Her attackers told her to keep her mouth shut and threatened her with continued attacks if she kept complaining. Guards implicated in these abuses were simply transferred to another facility; no disciplinary action was taken. None of the guards or inmates involved was ever charged with a crime. A civil lawsuit for compensation was settled in Robin Lucas' favour in 1998.[60]

Transgender women may also be at heightened risk of ill-treatment, particularly if they are placed in male prisons or jails. In order to ensure their protection, transgender prisoners should be held in accommodation appropriate for their preferred gender identity. In some cases the best interests of the prisoner may be better served by segregation from non-transgender inmates. However, segregation in prisons should avoid further marginalizing transgender people within the prison community or rendering them at further risk of torture or ill-treatment. The line between prisoner protection and homophobic discrimination is easily blurred by the prison authorities, and prison officials can sometimes conceal their discriminatory behaviour, and remain unaccountable for their actions, by claiming that they are acting to protect LGBT prisoners.

In February 1999, three guards at Fleury-Merogis prison in Essonne, France, were sentenced to four years' imprisonment (one of which was suspended) for sexual assaults against transgender prisoners held in a wing of the prison reportedly reserved for sexual minority prisoners.[61] The abuses first came to light in 1996 when a detainee complained to the prison doctor that she had been raped by a guard. During a visit to the prison in October 1996, the European Committee for the Prevention of Torture and Inhuman or Degrading Treatment or Punishment was informed by prisoners that guards routinely blackmailed them into having sex. The Committee immediately informed the French authorities, who opened a judicial investigation.[62] In its report following the visit, the Committee said it was assured of the French authorities' commitment to prevent and punish such cases of "ill-treatment" and made no reference to the fact that the prisoners were transgender.[63] However, the local prison workers' union criticized the lack of guidelines, training and specialized structures for dealing with transgender prisoners.[64] The prison psychiatrist was reported as saying that abuses against transgender people in prison would only be prevented by improving their material conditions.[65] Charges of aggravated rape were reportedly dropped when one of the victims, who had reported being gang-raped, refused to testify on the grounds that their family had received threats.[66]

Den homo-
sexuellen
NS-
Opfern

und
Lesben
vom
Sonntags-
Club
und
Mann
-O-
Meter

4: FORCED MEDICAL TREATMENT IN STATE INSTITUTIONS

Torture and ill-treatment of LGBT people have been reported in various other state institutions, such as hospitals and other health care facilities, and the military. In some societies, homosexuality is treated as a medical or psychological disorder and lesbians and gay men have been targeted for medical experimentation and forced psychiatric treatment designed to "cure" their homosexuality.

Although homosexuality is not currently criminalized in Russia, until recently male homosexuality was punishable by law. Lesbianism, by contrast, has tended to be treated as a mental disorder warranting psychiatric treatment. The police are known to have placed lesbians in psychiatric hospitals against their will solely on the grounds of their sexual orientation – sometimes at the request of family members or friends.[67]

Alla Pitcherskaia, a lesbian from Russia, alleged that she had been repeatedly charged with the crime of "hooliganism" and detained by the Russian militia because of her sexual orientation. While in detention, Alla Pitcherskaia was threatened with being placed in a psychiatric institution if she continued her work with a lesbian youth organization. She was also pressed to name lesbian and gay friends, and beaten. When Alla Pitcherskaia visited her girlfriend, who was being forcibly held in a psychiatric institution, she was herself registered as a "suspected lesbian" and told to go to her local clinic for outpatient sessions. When Alla Pitcherskaia failed to attend these sessions, she received written "Demands for Appearance" threatening her with forced institutionalization.

Alla Pitcherskaia fled to the USA where she lodged an application for asylum. Her application was initially rejected by the US Board of Immigration Appeals, in part because they claimed

A wreath in the shape of a pink triangle, the sign homosexuals were forced to wear by the Nazi authorities, commemorates the deaths of gay people at the former Sachsenhausen concentration camp, Germany. The wreath was laid in 1999.

© Daphne Scholinksi

Ghosts That Haunt Her, artwork by Daphne Scholinksi, a woman who was placed by her parents in a psychiatric institution in Chicago, USA, when she was 15 years old. Inappropriately diagnosed with gender identity disorder because of her gender presentation and perceived sexual orientation, she spent the next three years in a number of institutions. Her treatment included drug therapy, physical restraint and other forms of humiliating ill-treatment.

More can be learned about her experiences in her memoir, "The Last Time I Wore A Dress" (published by Penguin/Putnam). Daphne Scholinksi can be contacted via e-mail at *Lastdress@aol.com* Artwork cannot be reproduced without the artist's permission.

the motive for the forced itutionalization was the desire to "treat" or "cure" and not to punish and therefore was not "persecution". However, a federal court reversed the Board's decision, ruling that "'punishment' is neither a mandatory nor sufficient aspect of persecution" and that "persecution simply requires that the perpetrator cause the victim suffering or harm. Human rights laws cannot be sidestepped by simply couching actions that torture mentally or physically in benevolent terms such as 'curing' or 'treating' the victims."[68]

Threats of punitive psychiatric treatment are reported to have been used more recently by police in neighbouring Ukraine. According to the gay rights organization *Nash Mir,* in October 2000 police raided a bar in Kiev frequented by gay men. Police officers reportedly forced those in the bar to stand facing the wall for four hours and threatened them with compulsory psychiatric examinations before letting the men go.

In the 1970s and 1980s, "suspected" gay men and lesbians in the South African Defense Force (SADF) were forced to undergo "conversion therapy" and other forms of "treatment" without their informed consent.[69] In violation of both human rights and sound public health principles, they "were subjected to physical and psychological torture, experimentation and general gross maltreatment, including aversion therapy and chemical castration."[70] Those responsible for carrying out such practices included both military and health professionals. Aversion therapy sometimes involved applying electric current, via electrodes, to men while they were shown pictures of naked men. The current would be turned off when photographs of naked women were substituted for those of men.[71] AI has supported the call for the appointment of a commission of inquiry into these allegations of gross human rights violations.

Challenging the official characterization of homosexuality as an illness is an essential step towards ending ill-treatment of LGBT people. In 1992 the World Health Organization (WHO), a UN agency, removed homosexual orientation from its International Classification of Diseases.[72] Some national medical and psychiatric associations have taken steps, albeit slowly, to bring their policy into line with that of the WHO.

In China, where homosexuality was for many years a completely taboo subject, recent years have seen greater openness regarding issues relating to sexual orientation. One manifestation of this change has been the decision by the Chinese Psychiatric Association that the Chinese Classification of Mental Disorders Third Division will delete homosexuality from the list of mental disorders in April 2001.[73]

5: 'THE SEVERITY SHOWS THE HATRED' — HOMOPHOBIC VIOLENCE IN THE COMMUNITY

"They locked me in a room and brought him everyday to rape me so I would fall pregnant and be forced to marry him. They did this to me until I was pregnant..."

This account of rape and forced pregnancy may have chilling echoes of the violence against women committed during the recent conflicts in the Balkans or central Africa. But this act of torture was not committed in custody or in armed conflict — it happened to a teenage girl at her "peaceful" family home in Zimbabwe. Those who ordered the rape were not enemy military commanders — they were the girl's own parents, who were so determined to "correct" their daughter's lesbianism that they forced her to be repeatedly raped by an older man.[74]

Much of the violence faced by lesbian and gay people occurs within the community or in the family. As with torture by state officials, violence in the community is intentionally used to punish, to intimidate and to enforce discrimination against LGBT people. Like torture in custody, such violence is sometimes fatal and its consequences are always devastating.

While LGBT people are most likely to experience physical and psychological abuse at the hands of their parents, relatives, schoolmates, colleagues or individuals and groups from the community in which they live, this does not absolve the state of responsibility.

"Homophobia kills!" A vigil for Edson Neris Da Silva where he was beaten to death by skinheads in São Paulo, Brazil, in February 2000. Brazilian LGBT rights activists report that homophobic attacks and murders have gone uninvestigated. The conviction of two skinheads in February 2001 for the attack on Edson Da Silva marked a significant break with this pattern of impunity.

State responsibility for violence in the community

The extent to which governments share responsibility for "private" acts of torture or ill-treatment varies according to the context. In some cases, violence is instigated by officials at the highest level. In other cases, government tolerance of homophobic violence may rise to the level of complicity or acquiescence.

States' obligation to exercise due diligence

The term "due diligence" describes a threshold of efforts which a state must undertake to fulfil its responsibility to protect individuals from abuses of their rights. The UN Special Rapporteur on violence against women, its causes and consequences, has held that a "[s]tate can be held complicit where it fails systematically to provide protection from private actors who deprive any person of his/her human rights".[75]

A state cannot, for example, avoid responsibility for the routine ill-treatment of domestic workers by arguing that the abuse takes place in the privacy of the employers' homes, or that it was justified by social or cultural practices. Due diligence includes taking effective steps to prevent such abuses, to investigate them when they occur, to prosecute the alleged perpetrators and bring them to justice through fair proceedings, and to provide adequate compensation and other forms of redress. It also means ensuring that justice is dispensed without discrimination of any kind.

The standard of due diligence was articulated by the Inter-American Court of Human Rights which stated: "An illegal act which violates human rights and which is initially not directly imputable to the State (for example, because it is an act of a private person or because the person responsible has not been identified) can lead to international responsibility of the State, not because of the act itself but because of the lack of due diligence to prevent the violation or to respond to it as required by the Convention."[76] The Court also stated: "The State has a legal duty to take reasonable steps to prevent human rights violations and to use the means at its disposal to carry out a serious investigation of violations committed within its jurisdiction, to identify those responsible, to impose the appropriate punishment and to ensure the victim receives adequate compensation."[77]

The European Court of Human Rights has also affirmed that states are required to take measures to ensure that individuals are not subjected to torture or inhuman or degrading treatment or punishment, including such ill-treatment inflicted by private individuals. In 1998, the Court found that the United Kingdom had violated Article 3 of the European Convention on Human Rights (prohibiting torture and ill-treatment) by failing to provide adequate protection to a nine-year-old boy beaten with a cane by his stepfather.[78]

State inaction can be seen in a range of different areas. These include inadequate preventive measures; police indifference to abuses; bias against non-heterosexual forms of sexuality in the court system; failure to define abuses as criminal offences; and legal loopholes which hamper criminal prosecution. Most LGBT victims of violence find access to legal redress and reparations difficult, if not impossible. Impunity and indifference habitually surround many acts of violence against LGBT people.

In Zimbabwe, for example, President Robert Mugabe has for years conducted a campaign of virulent hate speech against lesbians and gay men, going as far as to say "I don't believe that they have any rights at all."[79] When the organization Gays and Lesbians of Zimbabwe (GALZ) organized a stall at the Harare bookfair in 1996, they were threatened and their stall was set alight by a pro-government student group. Police looked on and refused to give GALZ protection, arguing that they had brought the attacks on themselves.

The Jamaica Forum for Lesbians, All Sexuals and Gays (J-FLAG) has described how laws penalizing same-sex relations in Jamaica give official sanction to the many acts of violence committed against LGBT people. One young man whose gay relationship was discovered by family members was chased into a church by armed local residents who shot him dead as he begged for his life. Although the cruelty of the attack provoked outrage, the "spirit" of the act was widely commended. His partner left home after receiving death threats and was allegedly refused police protection. According to reports, gay men who report attacks to the police are at best met with indifference and at worst face further victimization.

Even in countries where there is no such degree of state incitement or tolerance of anti-gay hate crimes, the authorities can fail to exercise due diligence in preventing attacks, investigating them when they occur and ensuring that the perpetrators are brought to justice. Organizations monitoring anti-gay violence in the USA have noted that despite an apparent rise in reported homophobic attacks, the police response is often inadequate or even hostile, with few cases leading to the conviction of the perpetrators.

Viewed against this backdrop of state action and inaction, homophobic violence in the community becomes a human rights issue engaging the state's responsibility under international standards relating to torture and ill-treatment. From the perspective of international law, violence by non-state actors was traditionally divorced conceptually from torture and ill-treatment by agents of the state. From the perspective of the victim, their effects are often inseparable.

© Vincenzo Pinto/Reuters

IL COLOSSEO AI GAY? CON I LEONI DENTRO

Irina,[80] a Russian lesbian, claimed asylum in the USA on the grounds that she had been tortured or ill-treated by a range of people, including police, private investigators and her own family members. Irina described how in 1995 her sisters demanded she give up custody of her son and get psychiatric treatment to "cure" her of her homosexuality. Her mother threatened to disclose her sexual orientation to the authorities unless she gave up her son. Irina's parents hired two investigators to probe into her lifestyle. The investigators claimed to have a video tape of Irina having sex with her partner and threatened to report her to the police unless she paid a large sum of money. Irina and her lover went to the police to report this attempt to blackmail them; the officer responded by sexually harassing them. One day, the investigators abducted her at knife point and took her to an apartment. Together with another man, they raped Irina to "teach her a lesson" and "reorientate" her sexual identity. Irina decided not to report the rape to the police because of her past experience at their hands.[81]

Members of the neo-fascist organization, *Forza Nuova*, demonstrating against the hosting of World Pride, the first global LGBT Pride gathering, in Rome, July 2000. The banner reads: "Give the Colosseum to the gays? Only if the lions are in it." *Forza Nuova* had threatened violence against Pride participants in the weeks before the event. LGBT activists accused the Vatican of fostering a climate of intolerance after the Vatican opposed the timing of the World Pride event during the Roman Catholic Church's Holy Year Jubilee and dubbed it a "provocation".

Lesbians at risk in the home and community

The prevalence in society at large of sexism and homophobia creates a climate where lesbians are at grave risk of abuse in the community and home. Young lesbians who disclose their sexual orientation are sometimes forced by their families into marriages or other sexual relationships with men. Forcing women and girls into marriage or other relationships involving repeated non-consensual sex is not only discriminatory, it can amount to torture and sexual slavery. Lesbians are sometimes at risk of ill-treatment in ways which gay or bisexual men are not, for instance in forced virginity examinations, or forced pregnancy. Because women's sexual experience can more easily be controlled by the family and the community, lesbians may face a different range of obstacles in resisting ill-treatment or seeking redress. Women who are attracted to other women, whether they define themselves as lesbians or not, are at risk of ill-treatment in societies where they are viewed as bringing "shame" on their families or communities.

In some countries the media shares responsibility for fostering a climate of intolerance which can easily lead to violence. In August 1999, in Sri Lanka, where homosexuality is punishable by up to 12 years in prison, *The Island* newspaper published a letter protesting against a lesbian conference which was to be held in Colombo. The author called for police to "let loose convicted rapists among the jubilant but jaded jezebels when their assembly is in full swing so that those who are misguided may get a taste of the real thing." Companions on a Journey, a Sri Lankan lesbian and gay organization, lodged a complaint about the letter with the Sri Lankan Press Council. However, the Press Council refused to condemn the newspaper and ruled that the author had the right to offer his point of view, and that his view was justified because lesbianism is an "act of sadism", and was an offence under the country's penal code. The Press Council also stated that lesbianism is "at least an act of gross indecency" and "unnatural" and that "misguided and erratic women should be corrected and allowed to understand the true sense and reality of life."[82]

The UN Special Rapporteur on violence against women has noted that "A woman who is perceived to be acting in a manner deemed to be sexually inappropriate by communal standards is liable to be punished. In most communities, the option available to women for sexual activity is confined to marriage with a man from the same community. Women who choose options which are disapproved of by the community, whether to have a sexual relationship with a man in a non-marital relationship, to have such a relationship outside of ethnic, religious or class communities, or to live out their sexuality in ways other than

Activists demonstrate in New Delhi, India, in support of the Hindu film, *Fire*, which depicts a sexual relationship between two women, December 1998. The film was heavily criticized by some leading members of the *Shiv Sena* party and prompted attacks by party members on cinemas showing the film.

heterosexuality, are often subjected to violence and degrading treatment... States have an affirmative obligation to confront those cultural practices of the community which result in violence against women and which degrade and humiliate women, thereby denying them the full enjoyment of their rights. International standards require that there be concerted State policy to eradicate practices even if their proponents argue that they have their roots in religious beliefs and rituals."[83] AI believes that this applies to all gender-based violence defended for cultural reasons, including violence against LGBT people.

Young people at risk

Young people who show signs, or who are perceived as showing signs, of same-sex attraction are often at risk of violence in the home and community, the first expressions of their sexual identity sometimes attracting brutal chastisement. There are numerous cases of young lesbians being beaten, raped and attacked by family members — to punish, to break their spirit, to make it clear that their minds and bodies are not free.[84] The effects on young people of all forms of torture or ill-treatment and the consequences for their overall social and emotional development are particularly acute.

For many LGBT people, memories of the schoolyard evoke little nostalgia:

"I was in the middle of the parking lot of my school, and a group of [boys] surrounded me. They said, 'Let's string up the fag and tie him to the back of our truck and drag him down the highway.' They took a lasso out and started throwing it around my neck... All I can remember is being surrounded by these people, and how I was scared to death for my life."[85]

In January 2000, Derek Henkle brought a civil rights action against education officials in Nevada, USA, claiming that they had repeatedly and wilfully failed to take action against continuous and severe ill-treatment by other students at three different schools between 1995 and 1997. Rather than addressing the harmful behaviour of the culprits, Derek Henkle was moved from school to school before leaving the public school system altogether at the age of 16 without finishing his studies.

Although the treatment Derek Henkle was subjected to reflects that of many young people at risk, the fact that he has been able to pursue redress is unusual. Most children feel unable to report the abuse inflicted on them to their teachers or families, let alone seek redress from the education authorities through the courts.

A young gay Syrian man who was granted asylum in the USA in 2000 described his adolescence as "full of pain and mistreatment". He claimed that in 1994 he was held back after school and raped by a teacher who told him he was "a sin to this world". He fled to Jordan, where in 1999 he was again sexually assaulted. When he complained to the Jordanian police, they taunted him and refused to help him, threatening to put him "somewhere scary" if he ever bothered them again. He became suicidal and decided to reveal his sexual orientation to his parents. "My father became enraged and start[ed] hitting me and kicking me saying that I was degrading his family name... [he] threw me out in the street."[86]

The UN Convention on the Rights of the Child explicitly obliges states to protect all children — without distinction of any kind — against violence and other abuse in the home, at school and in the community. As with domestic violence against women, violence against children in the home or at school not only damages the body, it has a long-lasting and devastating effect on the child's sense of dignity and self-worth. Failure to protect children at risk because of their real or perceived sexual identity is perhaps one of the cruellest forms of homophobic discrimination and violation of their rights.

Extending protection

The failure of the authorities in many countries to protect LGBT people against violence in the community has led to the creation of organizations working to monitor and prevent such violence. Anti-violence projects in a number of countries have documented patterns of hate-motivated physical attacks and have made recommendations to the authorities regarding the effective monitoring and investigation of homophobic violence.

These organizations have highlighted the particular viciousness and brutality of violent crimes fuelled by

© AP

homophobia. As a 1997 report by the Southern Poverty Law Center in the USA commented: "When gays and lesbians are attacked it's particularly vicious... They aren't just punched. They're punched and kicked. They're beat and spit on. They're tied up and dragged behind cars. It's almost as if the attacker is trying to rub out the gay person's entire identity."

A key element in protecting LGBT people from torture and ill-treatment is putting an end to the impunity enjoyed by their attackers. In November 2000, a mob of around 200 armed people attacked a conference in Yogyakarta, Indonesia, attended by over 350 people working in the field

Brandon Teena, born female and named Teena Brandon, was living as a man in preparation for sex-change surgery when he was murdered in Nebraska, USA, in 1993. Reportedly "outed" to the local press by the police, he was subsequently raped and a few days later murdered with two other young people, Lisa Lambert and Philip Devine. Of two men convicted of the murders, one is currently appealing against the death penalty; another is serving three life sentences. Brandon Teena's family has initiated legal action against the police for failing to arrest the attackers after the rape was reported.

of sexual health and reproductive rights. Participants included representatives of Indonesian LGBT organizations as well as health workers and lesbian, gay, bisexual and transgender people from Yogyakarta. This attack took place in the context of an increased number of attacks by radical Muslim groups against a range of targets which included bars and discotheques, as well as events such as the Yogyakarta conference. At least 10 people were injured and several required hospital treatment. According to eyewitnesses, the attackers forced their way into the conference building and began terrorizing the participants with clubs, swords, chairs and iron bars.

Indonesia's weak and corrupt judicial system routinely fails victims of both ordinary crimes and human rights violations. In this case, the police reportedly questioned around 57 suspects after the attack, but released them all shortly afterwards without pressing charges. Angered by the failure of the police to conduct further investigations, activists and lawyers in Yogyakarta set up a People's Anti-Violence Committee to launch their own legal proceedings in an attempt to bring the perpetrators to justice. One of the organizers of the conference told AI: "The attack has sent shockwaves through the gay community here. It just doesn't feel safe any more... The attackers must be brought to justice to show that this kind of violence will not be tolerated."

Anti-violence projects in Australia have highlighted that prevention of ill-treatment needs to focus on attitudes in society as a whole, not just on the perpetrator of the crime.[87] Violence is a manifestation of deeply ingrained prejudice often reinforced through laws or official policies which stigmatize homosexual behaviour.

The link between discrimination and violence in the community was highlighted by the nail-bombing of a pub frequented by gay people in central London in April 1999. The bombing clearly revealed the links between racism and homophobia, and the interrelated nature of all discrimination based on identity. Two earlier bombs had exploded in parts of London with a large black and Asian population. At his trial the man responsible for all three bombs, a neo-Nazi sympathizer, explained why he had selected the three sites: "First of all it was gonna be the blacks, then the Asians, then queers." He was sentenced to life imprisonment.

6: FLEEING TORTURE BASED ON SEXUAL IDENTITY

In the absence of effective protection against torture and other violations, many LGBT people are forced to flee their country in search of physical safety. However, LGBT people face specific obstacles in claiming asylum and having their claims recognized.

To be recognized as a refugee under the 1951 UN Convention relating to the Status of Refugees, a person must prove that they have a well-founded fear of persecution for reasons of race, religion, nationality, membership of a particular social group or political opinion. It is the policy of the UN High Commissioner for Refugees (UNHCR) that people facing attack, inhumane treatment, or serious discrimination because of their homosexuality and whose governments are unable or unwilling to protect them should be recognized as refugees.[88] In 1995, the UNHCR determined that lesbians and gay men did comprise a "particular social group" and so could be granted refugee status on that basis under the terms of the UN Refugee Convention where they had a well-founded fear of persecution. The UN Convention against Torture prohibits the return of anyone, without exception, to a country where they could be at risk of torture. There are now at least 18 countries which have granted asylum to people fleeing persecution based on sexual orientation.[89]

Yet despite the protection enshrined in international law, many factors prevent people who have been persecuted on the basis of their sexual orientation from getting international protection.

Lesbians and gay men who have experienced torture or ill-treatment may not have access to documented evidence of their personal experiences. Patterns of torture and other abuses facing lesbians and gay men are not well documented in most countries, although some non-governmental organizations have begun to track these abuses. In addition many people are reluctant to reveal their sexual orientation to immigration officials – particularly if they are fleeing persecution by state officials because of their sexual identities. LGBT people may not reveal intimate details about their lives for fear of not being

Phumi Mtetwa, Co-Secretary General of the International Lesbian and Gay Association, and Surina Khan, Executive Director of the International Gay and Lesbian Human Rights Commission, speaking at a "Sexual Rights are Human Rights" panel at the 23rd Special Session of the UN General Assembly on "Women 2000: Gender Equality, Development and Peace for the 21st Century" (the Beijing+5 conference), New York, June 2000.

taken seriously, of being overtly mocked, of having their confidentiality compromised, or of additional abuse.

When LGBT people are seeking asylum in countries where homosexual relations are criminalized they are not likely to pursue claims based on their "illegal" behaviour or identities; to do so would immediately put them at risk of scrutiny or suspicion, and quite possibly of further persecution.

Many refugees and their legal representatives are not aware that the option of filing an asylum claim on the grounds of persecution because of their sexual orientation is available to them. Reluctance to file a claim on this basis for a host of reasons, including fear of reprisals, can result in applicants being disqualified, irrespective of the merits of the case. For example, a Honduran man claiming asylum in the USA feared speaking openly to immigration officials. He omitted key details of the homophobic ill-treatment he was fleeing because he feared that fellow inmates in the immigration detention centre would turn violent if he disclosed his sexual orientation. The fear of disclosure and potential breaches of confidentiality were so great that this asylum-seeker chose to censor some of the most important supporting information for his claim. The claim was rejected.[90]

Immigration officials are often not trained in how to sensitively solicit information about persecution related to sexuality. The authorities may also lack awareness about particular forms of harm that are specific to LGBT people – such as forced psychiatric treatment as a "cure" for homosexuality – and may therefore fail to recognize such abuse as persecution for the purposes of the UN Refugee Convention.

Factors such as gender, race, age and ethnicity can also affect the treatment of asylum-seekers by officials. As a gay man from Pakistan who sought and received asylum in the USA commented, "The asylum process requires the painting of one's own country in extremely racist and colonialist ways in order to show its homophobia."[91]

This combination of obstacles, social stigma and discrimination means that the torture and ill-treatment of lesbian and gay people are under-reported, poorly documented and too often rendered invisible. The result is that people in need of asylum are denied protection.

Lesbians and gay men may suffer further ill-treatment after fleeing their home countries, no matter what the basis of their claims. In a number of countries asylum-seekers are often held in detention centres or prisons while their claims are being reviewed. Asylum-seekers sometimes spend years in prison waiting for their claims to be adjudicated. While in detention they may be subjected to torture or ill-treatment by guards and officials, as well as other detainees.

A gay man from Indonesia was detained in the El Paso Service Processing Center unit, a detention facility of the Immigration and Naturalization Service (INS) in the USA, for over two years, between 1998 and 2000. He was locked up because he was gay and had fled his home after receiving death threats and other threats from groups that accused him of "shaming" them. While held in detention, he experienced persistent homophobic verbal harassment by officers in the facility. He was told he would be transferred to a prison "for his own safety" or placed in the Special Housing Unit, the solitary confinement area of the detention centre, where detainees are kept, allegedly "when the INS feels that it cannot protect a detainee."[92]

Despite the range of obstacles facing LGBT people in their asylum claims, there have been significant advances in the asylum landscape in recent years. There is increasing agreement within the international community that people fleeing torture and ill-treatment for reasons of sexual identity, including homophobic violence in the community, may qualify as refugees under the UN Refugee Convention.

In 1995 the Refugee Status Appeal Authority in New Zealand ruled that "recognition is given to the principle that refugee law ought to concern itself with actions which deny human dignity in any key way... On this interpretation, the issue of sexual orientation presents little difficulty. As we have earlier remarked, sexual orientation is a characteristic which is either innate or unchangeable or so fundamental to identity or to human dignity that the individual should not be forced to forsake or change the characteristic."[93]

In 1997, the Latvian Centre for Refugees, which is part of the Ministry of the Interior, claimed that even though lesbians and gay men are not specifically mentioned in the country's refugee law, the Centre would closely follow UNHCR's interpretation of the phrase "social group" and its inclusion of sexual orientation. Well-founded fear of persecution based on sexual orientation could be proved when homosexual acts are totally banned, when homosexual people are persecuted or their rights violated by the state authorities, or by other individuals where the state fails to provide adequate protection.[94]

In May 2000, South Africa was added to the list of countries which have extended asylum to people fleeing persecution based on sexual orientation when it adopted a new Refugee Act. By January 2000, four gay men — two from Pakistan and one each from Uganda and Zambia — had submitted applications for asylum in anticipation of the new law.[95]

In August 2000, a US federal court ordered the US government to grant asylum to Giovanni Hernandez-Montiel, a transgender Mexican gay man who had been arrested, detained, strip-searched, raped and otherwise tortured by Mexican police over a period of years. The Court ruled that "this case is about sexual identity, not fashion" and held that "gay men who have female sexual identities in Mexico constitute a particular social group for asylum purposes" and that Giovanni Hernandez-Montiel should be granted asylum based on his well-founded fear of persecution.[96] This marked the first time that a US federal court had granted asylum based on sexual orientation.

7: 'FIGHTING FOR OUR LIVES' – HUMAN RIGHTS DEFENDERS

Until relatively recently the silence and indifference surrounding the torture and ill-treatment of lesbian, gay, bisexual and transgender people was reflected in the work of much of the international human rights community. While the work of organizations such as AI focused public attention on the plight of imprisoned political dissidents, those persecuted as sexual or emotional "dissidents" remained largely forgotten victims. Issues of sexuality and sexual orientation rarely figured on the agendas of international governmental organizations and the human rights mechanisms of the UN.

However, the conspiracy of silence surrounding violations of lesbian and gay rights has now been broken. Over the last three decades, movements have emerged in countries all over the globe to defend the human rights of LGBT people. They have campaigned for an end to police brutality, for the decriminalization of homosexuality and for equal protection before the law in the face of homophobic violence and discrimination. These activists have won some impressive victories, winning legal reforms and bringing about changes in cultural attitudes.

Lesbian, gay and bisexual issues began to be articulated in a public forum in India in the late 1980s with the founding of India's first gay magazine, *Bombay Dost*, and the creation of a lesbian collective in Delhi called Sakhi. Today there are organizations, helplines, newsletters, health resources, social spaces and drop-in centres in most major cities in India. Reports of a sharp increase in attacks on LGBT people in Bangalore, including police ill-treatment, led to the formation of the Coalition for Sexuality Minorities' Rights, comprising LGBT, lawyers' and women's organizations, and social activists. The Coalition approached a human rights group, the People's Union for Civil Liberties — Karnataka (PUCL-K), to help investigate and mobilize public opinion against such abuses "in an attempt to break through the invisibility and the silence that society has tried to throw over people simply because of their sexual orientation."[97]

© AI

Transgender activist Melike Demir is one of eight transgender people who lodged official complaints of torture and ill-treatment against the police in Turkey. On 26 January 2001 the trial began of a chief commissioner accused of having tortured them in 1996 and 1997.

Melike Demir, a Turkish transgender activist and a former prisoner of conscience, takes part in AI's campaign to mark the 50th anniversary of the Universal Declaration of Human Rights, United Kingdom, 1998.

The eight spoke of the threats they had been subjected to, apparently in order to make them withdraw their complaints. Eren Keskin, Chairperson of the Istanbul branch of the Human Rights Association, described how she had confronted the commissioner some years earlier about similar reports of torture against transgender people. "He said, 'until today you were concerned about terrorists and now you deal with this lot, that are not human beings?' I told him that nobody deserved to be tortured."

© Companions on a Journey, Sri Lanka

Sherman de Rose and other members of Companions on a Journey, an LGBT organization in Sri Lanka, protesting outside a government ministry. In 2000 they campaigned against a Press Council ruling which failed to condemn a newspaper for publishing a call to rape lesbians. In February 2001 they received the Felipa de Souza Award from the International Gay and Lesbian Human Rights Commission for their contribution to the struggle for human rights.

In other countries organizations have been set up to monitor and prevent violence against LGBT people in the broader community. The first ever international conference on anti-gay hate crimes is due to take place in Sydney, Australia, in 2002, hosted by the New South Wales Coalition of Anti-Violence Projects. The conference aims to explore comprehensive approaches to violence against LGBT people using a human rights framework. The conference is an opportunity to promote awareness of the fact that violence against LGBT people, whether in custody, in the community or in the home, can constitute torture or ill-treatment which governments are obliged under international human rights standards to prevent, investigate and punish.

Perhaps the most enduring victory of the LGBT rights movement is that, at the start of the 21st century, lesbian and gay rights are finding a voice across the globe. Lesbian, gay, bisexual and transgender rights defenders are everywhere. There are scores of organizations in Africa, Asia, Latin America and the Middle East working for LGBT rights. These movements are forging their own language to claim rights of sexual identity. Their very existence challenges the lie of those who claim that homosexuality is "not part of our culture".

LGBT people have been active in local and national movements in fighting to defend human rights all over the world. They have been part of the struggle for women's rights. They have been anti-apartheid activists. They have campaigned for the "disappeared" in Latin America and the former Yugoslavia. Just as lesbian and gay people have taken part in countless campaigns on a whole range of human rights issues, so too the struggle to protect the human rights of LGBT people should be one that is waged by all.

LGBT rights defenders at risk

However, increased visibility has also brought renewed attacks on LGBT rights defenders, particularly in countries where the emergence of an LGBT rights movement is more recent. "Why this sudden hatred of homosexuals?", asks Indian LGBT rights activist Ashok Row Kavi. "Because it has become a political identity. Governments are trying to suppress it because they see it as a socially disruptive force."

In some countries where homosexuality is criminalized, LGBT rights advocacy may be considered incitement to commit a crime. Zambian Vice-President Christon Tembo has said: "An association formed to further the interests of homosexuals can never be registered in Zambia. Those who will persist in championing the cause of homosexual activities in Zambia risk being arrested for the felonies of committing criminal acts or for conspiracy to commit criminal acts."[98] The Zambian Lesbian, Gay and Transgender Association (LEGATRA) has reported that it has been refused official registration and so has been unable to carry out a public awareness campaign and challenge the ban on gay male sex. A former chair of LEGATRA is reported to have been attacked twice.

Poliyana Mangwiro and Keith Goddard of Gays and Lesbians of Zimbabwe (GALZ). GALZ members have faced harassment, including threats of violence and criminal prosecution, for their work in defence of the rights of lesbian and gay Zimbabweans.

The particular risks faced by human rights defenders working on issues of sexual orientation have been recognized by the Special Representative of the UN Secretary-General on human rights defenders. In her report to the Commission on Human Rights in March 2001 she stated: "Greater risks are faced by defenders of the rights of certain groups as their work challenges social structures, traditional practices and interpretation of religious precepts that may have been used over long periods of time to condone and justify violation of the human rights of members of such groups. Of special importance will be women's human rights groups and those who are active on issues of sexuality especially sexual orientation and reproductive rights. These groups are often very vulnerable to prejudice, to

© Vanessa Baird/New Internationalist

"There is no doubt that without this pressure they would not have given us police protection." In El Salvador, William Hernandez, director of the non-governmental organization *Entre Amigos*, which works with sexual minorities and provides sexual health education, received death threats in 1999 and the *Entre Amigos* offices were raided by unidentified persons. Requests for police protection were only granted after international pressure.

marginalization and to public repudiation, not only by State forces but other social actors."99

An important first step for others in the international human rights movement will be to recognize that those campaigning against torture, ill-treatment and for an end to violence and discrimination against LGBT people are indeed human rights defenders, working to realize the promise of the Universal Declaration of Human Rights — that all are equal in dignity and rights.

Being able to count on the cooperation of the broader human rights community can be a vital safeguard for LGBT human rights defenders, and an important means of combating attempts to undermine the legitimacy of their work and to marginalize them. In the words of Juan Pablo Ordoñez, a Colombian human rights defender: "The defence of human rights of homosexuals solely by homosexuals is impossible — or at best, places them in imminent peril of their lives. The struggle must be taken up by outsiders, gay or straight people, who are not themselves victims of this hostile society."

8: RECOMMENDATIONS

Drawing on years of experience of working against torture worldwide, AI has devised a 12-Point Program bringing together the most important measures which governments should take to prevent torture and ill-treatment by agents of the state (see Appendix).

AI's more recent research has highlighted the need for specific measures to protect those at risk because of their real or perceived sexual identity. These include additional preventive safeguards and steps for overcoming impunity and combating discrimination, two key factors behind the persistence of torture.

Most of the recommendations below are aimed at governments, who have the prime responsibility to end torture. Others are addressed to intergovernmental and non-governmental organizations.

Recommendations for governments

1. Repeal laws criminalizing homosexuality

Review all legislation which could result in the discrimination, prosecution and punishment of people solely for their sexual orientation or gender identity. This includes "sodomy" laws or similar provisions outlawing homosexual or transgender behaviour; discriminatory age of consent legislation; public order legislation used to prosecute and punish people solely for their sexual identity; and laws banning the "promotion" of homosexuality which can be used to imprison LGBT rights advocates.

All such laws should be repealed or amended. Anyone imprisoned or detained solely for their real or perceived sexual orientation or gender identity should be released immediately and unconditionally. This includes those detained for same-sex sexual relations between consenting adults in private, those held for advocating LGBT rights, and those detained for their political beliefs or activities under the pretext of charges of homosexuality.

Flogging, all other corporal punishments, the death penalty and all other cruel, inhuman and degrading punishments should be abolished in law.

2. Condemn torture, whoever the victim

Officials at the highest level should publicly condemn torture and make clear that any act of torture or ill-treatment, whoever the victim, will not be tolerated. They should ensure that they do not make any public statement or order which could reasonably be interpreted as a licence to torture or ill-treat people because of their sexual identity. Those who make such statements should be held accountable for instigating, inciting or abetting torture.

3. Provide safeguards in custody

Ensure that all law enforcement personnel, prison staff, medical personnel and other relevant officials are trained in how to protect lesbian, gay, bisexual and transgender people from torture or ill-treatment.

Take effective measures to prevent rape and other sexual violence against LGBT people in custody. Rape in police or prison custody should always be recognized as an act of torture. Women prisoners should be held separately from men prisoners. They should not be supervised by male members of staff and female security personnel should be present during their interrogation.

Segregation in prisons should avoid further marginalizing LGBT people within the prison community or rendering them at further risk of torture or ill-treatment. Transgender prisoners should normally be held in accommodation based on their preferred gender identity.

LGBT people in custody should have adequate access to medical care appropriate to their needs. Women should have access to female medical staff. Where conjugal visits are permitted, they should be granted on an equal basis to all prisoners and detainees, regardless of the sex of their partners.

The authorities should ensure that officials policing demonstrations, enforcing public order provisions, or maintaining order in places of detention adhere to international standards on the use of force and firearms.

4. Prohibit forced medical 'treatment'

Medical "treatment" of LGBT people against their will and aimed at changing their sexual orientation or gender identity is cruel, inhuman or degrading treatment which could amount to torture. It should be prohibited in all circumstances. The involvement of health professionals in such "treatment" violates international codes of medical ethics prohibiting their involvement in torture or ill-treatment.[100] National medical associations that have not yet done so should affirm that homosexuality is not a medical disorder and should condemn, and prohibit their members from participating in, any treatment aimed at "curing" or "treating" it.

5. End impunity

Ensure that all allegations and reports of torture or ill-treatment on account of real or perceived sexual identity are promptly and impartially investigated and those responsible brought to justice.

The authorities should establish effective independent mechanisms to monitor the actions of law enforcement and judicial officials to identify and eliminate all forms of discrimination in the criminal justice system, and remove any obstacles preventing those responsible for torture or ill-treatment being brought to justice.

The authorities should establish systems for effective consultation with relevant community groups, including LGBT human rights defenders. Monitoring bodies should maintain and publish comprehensive statistics and other documentation on complaints of homophobic violence, both by state officials and others.

Special measures should be implemented to ensure that people who have been victims of torture or ill-treatment based on sexual identity, including rape and other sexual abuse, have access to the means of gaining redress and the right to an effective remedy, including rehabilitation and compensation.

6. Protect LGBT people against violence in the community

Police and judicial authorities should act with due diligence to protect LGBT people against violence within the broader community, including domestic violence. The authorities should make clear that such violence is a criminal offence and will not be tolerated. Specific directives and training should be given to law enforcement officials on how to identify and investigate homophobic crimes. All allegations should be properly investigated, the perpetrators brought to justice and adequate redress provided to the victims.

Children too should be protected against physical and psychological violence inflicted on account of their real or perceived sexual identity. Educational authorities should implement policies to prevent homophobic assaults and other "bullying" in schools. Governments should honour their international obligations to protect children from all forms of violence in the home or in the community, including violence inflicted because of their real or perceived sexual identity.

Incitement to discrimination, hostility or violence against LGBT people should be prohibited, in accordance with the international standards prohibiting advocacy of hatred and anti-discrimination standards.[101]

7. Protect refugees fleeing torture based on sexual identity

Governments should review and amend asylum policies and practices so as to ensure that anyone with a well-founded fear of persecution on account of their real or imputed sexual identity is able to seek and obtain asylum in accordance with the UN Refugee Convention.

No one should be forcibly returned to a country where they risk persecution or torture, including states which would fail to protect them against persecution or torture in the community. The detention of asylum-seekers should normally be avoided.[102] In those limited circumstances where detention is lawful, the authorities should ensure that asylum-seekers are not subjected to torture or ill-treatment.

Guidelines should be issued to immigration officials and others involved in the asylum process for the sensitive handling of claims based on sexual orientation. Training should include how to eliminate bias in interviewing, documenting and accessing country-specific information, and should involve LGBT rights groups.

When assessing claims, country-specific information should be actively sought from LGBT, women's and other human rights organizations which document torture, ill-treatment and other abuses against LGBT people. Governments should monitor decisions for evidence of adverse discrimination; complaints should be properly investigated and fair and effective mechanisms of appeal should be made available.

8. Protect and support LGBT human rights defenders

Governments should ensure adequate protection of human rights defenders at risk because of their work on issues of gender and sexual identity. Their work should be supported and they should be consulted on policy initiatives to combat torture. Governments should remove legal and administrative obstacles which prevent LGBT rights defenders from carrying out their work; they should implement provisions of the UN Declaration on the Right and Responsibility of Individuals, Groups and Organs of Society to Promote and Protect Universally Recognized Human Rights and Fundamental Freedoms and the recommendations of the Special Representative of the UN Secretary-General on human rights defenders.

9. Strengthen international protection

States should ratify international instruments which provide for the prevention of torture and ill-treatment, without reservations. These include:

— International Covenant on Civil and Political Rights and its (first) Optional Protocol which recognizes the competence of the Human Rights Committee to consider individual complaints
— UN Convention against Torture and Other Cruel, Inhuman or Degrading Treatment or Punishment, including declarations under Articles 21 and 22 which recognize the competence of the Human Rights Committee to consider individual complaints, and without reservations
— UN Convention on the Elimination of All Forms of Discrimination against Women and its Optional Protocol which allows for the consideration of individual complaints;

— the International Covenant on Economic, Social and
Cultural Rights
— the International Convention on the Elimination of All Forms
of Racial Discrimination
— the UN Convention on the Rights of the Child
— the Rome Statute of the International Criminal Court
— relevant regional standards such as the Inter-American
Convention to Prevent and Punish Torture and the European
Convention for the Protection of Human Rights and
Fundamental Freedoms, including its newly adopted
Protocol 12 on discrimination, and the European Convention
for the Prevention of Torture and Inhuman or Degrading
Treatment or Punishment.

When submitting reports and communications to
international human rights bodies, governments should include
information on the steps being taken to protect LGBT people
against torture and ill-treatment, whether by state officials or
others in the community. Governments should implement the
recommendations of the special rapporteurs on violence against
women and on torture as a matter of priority.

Governments should ensure that protections for the human
rights of LGBT people are effectively advanced at all relevant UN
conferences and in the work of UN and regional human rights
bodies.

10. Combat discrimination

Governments should secure greater legal protection against
homophobic abuses by adopting constitutional and other
provisions prohibiting all forms of discrimination based on
sexual orientation or gender identity.

They should also promote diversity in the composition of
agencies responsible for the administration of justice, and
ensure that their anti-discrimination policies address issues of
sexual identity.

Governments should initiate and support public anti-
discrimination campaigns to raise awareness of the need to
protect the rights of all people, including LGBT people, to be
free from torture and ill-treatment. They should support the
work of organizations combating discrimination and enable

them to carry out their work without fear or unjustifiable restriction.

Restrictions on the freedom of association and peaceful assembly of LGBT organizations or individuals should not be applied in an arbitrary and discriminatory manner.

Recommendations for intergovernmental and non-governmental organizations

Existing UN human rights monitoring bodies should seek out information on torture, ill-treatment and other abuses based on sexual identity. Their work should include an analysis of patterns of torture and ill-treatment based on sexual identity and recommendations to address these, building on the work done by the UN special rapporteurs on torture, on violence against women, and on extrajudicial, summary or arbitrary executions; by the Special Representative of the UN Secretary-General on human rights defenders; and by the UN Human Rights Committee and the UN Committee on Economic, Social and Cultural Rights. These bodies should also promote examples of good practice among states.

The UN High Commissioner for Refugees should issue guidelines on asylum claims based on sexual orientation or gender identity, promoting awareness of best practice in certain jurisdictions.

Non-governmental organizations should strengthen their work in documenting and reporting human rights abuses against LGBT people. They should support victims of torture and their families, for example by submitting individual complaints to relevant government authorities and international human rights monitoring bodies. Urgent information on individuals facing torture should be sent for action to the UN Special Rapporteur on torture or the UN Special Rapporteur on violence against women, its causes and consequences.

APPENDIX: AI's 12-Point Program for the Prevention of Torture by Agents of the State

Amnesty International

12-Point Program for the Prevention of Torture by Agents of the State

Torture is a fundamental violation of human rights, condemned by the international community as an offence to human dignity and prohibited in all circumstances under international law.

Yet torture persists, daily and across the globe. Immediate steps are needed to confront torture and other cruel, inhuman or degrading treatment or punishment wherever they occur and to eradicate them totally.

Amnesty International calls on all governments to implement the following 12-Point Program for the Prevention of Torture by Agents of the State. It invites concerned individuals and organizations to ensure that they do so. Amnesty International believes that the implementation of these measures is a positive indication of a government's commitment to end torture and to work for its eradication worldwide.

1. Condemn torture
The highest authorities of every country should demonstrate their total opposition to torture. They should condemn torture unreservedly whenever it occurs. They should make clear to all members of the police, military and other security forces that torture will never be tolerated.

2. Ensure access to prisoners
Torture often takes place while prisoners are held incommunicado — unable to contact people outside who could help them or find out what is happening to them. The practice of incommunicado detention should be ended. Governments should ensure that all prisoners are brought before an independent judicial authority without delay after being taken into custody. Prisoners should have access to relatives, lawyers and doctors without delay and regularly thereafter.

3. No secret detention

In some countries torture takes place in secret locations, often after the victims are made to "disappear". Governments should ensure that prisoners are held only in officially recognized places of detention and that accurate information about their arrest and whereabouts is made available immediately to relatives, lawyers and the courts. Effective judicial remedies should be available to enable relatives and lawyers to find out immediately where a prisoner is held and under what authority and to ensure the prisoner's safety.

4. Provide safeguards during detention and interrogation

All prisoners should be immediately informed of their rights. These include the right to lodge complaints about their treatment and to have a judge rule without delay on the lawfulness of their detention. Judges should investigate any evidence of torture and order release if the detention is unlawful. A lawyer should be present during interrogations. Governments should ensure that conditions of detention conform to international standards for the treatment of prisoners and take into account the needs of members of particularly vulnerable groups. The authorities responsible for detention should be separate from those in charge of interrogation. There should be regular, independent, unannounced and unrestricted visits of inspection to all places of detention.

5. Prohibit torture in law

Governments should adopt laws for the prohibition and prevention of torture incorporating the main elements of the UN Convention against Torture and other Cruel, Inhuman or Degrading Treatment or Punishment (Convention against Torture) and other relevant international standards. All judicial and administrative corporal punishments should be abolished. The prohibition of torture and the essential safeguards for its prevention must not be suspended under any circumstances, including states of war or other public emergency.

6. Investigate

All complaints and reports of torture should be promptly, impartially and effectively investigated by a body independent of the alleged perpetrators. The methods and findings of such investigations should be made public. Officials suspected of committing torture should be suspended from active duty during the investigation. Complainants, witnesses and others at risk should be protected from intimidation and reprisals.

7. Prosecute

Those responsible for torture must be brought to justice. This principle should apply wherever alleged torturers happen to be, whatever their nationality or position, regardless of where the crime was committed and the nationality of the victims, and no matter how much time has elapsed since the commission of the crime. Governments must exercise universal jurisdiction over alleged torturers or extradite them, and cooperate with each other in such criminal proceedings. Trials must be fair. An order from a superior officer must never be accepted as a justification for torture.

8. No use of statements extracted under torture

Governments should ensure that statements and other evidence obtained through torture may not be invoked in any proceedings, except against a person accused of torture.

9. Provide effective training

It should be made clear during the training of all officials involved in the custody, interrogation or medical care of prisoners that torture is a criminal act. Officials should be instructed that they have the right and duty to refuse to obey any order to torture.

10. Provide reparation

Victims of torture and their dependants should be entitled to obtain prompt reparation from the state including restitution, fair and adequate financial compensation and appropriate medical care and rehabilitation.

11. Ratify international treaties

All governments should ratify without reservations international treaties containing safeguards against torture, including the UN Convention against Torture with declarations providing for individual and inter-state complaints. Governments should comply with the recommendations of international bodies and experts on the prevention of torture.

12. Exercise international responsibility

Governments should use all available channels to intercede with the governments of countries where torture is reported. They should ensure that transfers of training and equipment for military, security or police use do not facilitate torture. Governments must not forcibly return a person to a country where he or she risks being tortured.

This 12-Point Program was adopted by Amnesty International in October 2000 as a program of measures to prevent the torture and ill-treatment of people who are in governmental custody or otherwise in the hands of agents of the state. Amnesty International holds governments to their international obligations to prevent and punish torture, whether committed by agents of the state or by other individuals. Amnesty International also opposes torture by armed political groups.

ENDNOTES

1 Constitutional Court of South Africa, *NCGLE (National Coalition for Gay and Lesbian Equality)* v. *Minister of Justice*, CCT 11/98, 9 October 1998, paragraphs 126 and 127.

2 Statement given to Amnesty International, March 2000.

3 Not her real name. Pseudonyms have been used for all the Ugandan activists referred to in this chapter.

4 "Arrest Homos, says Museveni", *New Vision*, 28 September 1999.

5 "No easy escape to freedom", article sent to Amnesty International in May 2000.

6 Statement given to Amnesty International, October 1999.

7 Statement given to Amnesty International, March 2000.

8 Communications with Amnesty International, February and July 2000.

9 Namibia gay rights row, *BBC News, World Service, Africa*, 2 October 2000.

10 See for example, "Are homos NRM's new political ladder? Yes", *Sunday Monitor*, Uganda, 7 November 1999.

11 Human Rights Committee General Comment 20, 1992.

12 See for example, Articles 4(2) and 7 of the International Covenant on Civil and Political Rights.

13 Decisions of the European Court of Human Rights in *Dudgeon v. UK*, Series A No. 45, 1981, *Norris v. Republic of Ireland*, Series A No. 142, 1988, and *Modinos v. Cyprus*, Series A No. 259, 1993. See also Concluding Observations of the Human Rights Committee (Crown Dependencies): United Kingdom of Great Britain and Northern Ireland, UN Doc. CCPR/C/79/Add.119, 27 March 2000, para. 14; Concluding observations of the Human Rights Committee: Trinidad and Tobago, UN. Doc. CCPR/CO/70/TTO), 3 November 2000, para. 11; Concluding observations of the Human Rights Committee: Austria, UN Doc. CCPR/C/79/Add.103, 19 November 1998, para. 13.

14 Decisions of the European Court of Human Rights in *Dudgeon v. UK* (1981), *Norris v. Republic of Ireland* (1988) and *Modinos v. Cyprus* (1993).

15 Human Rights Committee, *Toonen v. Australia* (Views on Communication, No 488/1992, adopted 31 March 1994).

16 See for example: Concluding Observations of the Committee on the Rights of the Child (Isle of Man): United Kingdom of Great Britain and Northern Ireland, 16 October 2000, UN Doc. CRC/C/15/Add.134, para. 22; Concluding Observations of the Committee on the Elimination of Discrimination against Women: Kyrgyzstan, 27 January 1999, UN Doc. A/54/38, paras. 127-8; The right to the highest attainable standard of health (Article 12 of the International Covenant on Economic, Social and Cultural Rights): 11 August 2000, UN Doc. E/C.12/2000/4, CESCR General comment 14, para. 18.

17 *B v. France*, Series A, No. 232-C, 25 March 1992.

18 *P v. S and Cornwall County Council* (ECJ), European Court Reports 1996, I-2143.

19 See for example Human Rights Committee, Concluding Observations: Poland 29/07/99 (UN Doc. CCPR/C/79/Add.110), 29 July 1999, para. 23.

20 Luis Mott, *O Lesbianismo no Brasil*, Mercado Aberto, 1987.

21 *Breaking the Silence: Human rights violations based on sexual orientation*, Amnesty International UK Section, 1997; updated information from AI files.

22 In some countries where same-sex relations are not a criminal offence *per se*, discriminatory ages of consent laws may effectively criminalize behaviour which is perfectly legal for heterosexuals.

23 *Romania: Mariana Cetiner — Prisoner of conscience* (AI Index: EUR 39/030/1997); *Romania: AI appeals for the release of Mariana Cetiner* (AI Index: EUR 39/010/1998).

24 Mariana Cetiner, interview with Amnesty International, April 1998.

25 *Romania: Consensual homosexual relations continue to be punished under amended legislation* (AI Index: EUR 39/017/1996).

26 *Public Scandals: Sexual Orientation and the Criminal Law in Romania,* International Gay and Lesbian Human Rights Commission/Human Rights Watch, 1998.

27 Offences Against the Persons Act, Section 76.

28 Human Rights Committee, *Toonen v. Australia,* Communication, No 488/1992, para 8.5.

29 Penal Code, Section 377A and 377B.

30 See *Malaysia: Human Rights Undermined — Restrictive Laws in a Parliamentary Democracy* (AI Index: ASA 28/006/1999).

31 *Saudi Arabia: Further information on fear of flogging — Nine Saudi Arabian nationals* (AI Index: MDE 23/038/2000).

32 See for example, the case of Bariya Ibrahima Magazu, flogged in Nigeria for having sexual relations outside marriage after being unable to produce witnesses to substantiate her claim that she had been raped, in *Broken Bodies, Shattered Minds — Torture and ill-treatment of women* (AI Index: ACT 40/001/2001).

33 See *Afghanistan: Cruel, inhuman or degrading treatment or punishment* (AI Index: ASA 11/015/1999).

34 *United States of America: Allegations of homophobic abuse by Chicago police officers* (AI Index: AMR 51/022/2001).

35 Not her real name.

36 Statement given to Amnesty International, March 2001.

37 Bojan Aleksov, interview with Amnesty International.

38 *Argentina: Transvestite dies in detention* (AI Index: AMR 13/004/2000).

39 *Brazil: Possible Extrajudicial Executions/Fear for Safety* (AI Index: AMR 19/019/1997).

40 *Ecuador: Arbitrary detention of transvestites* (AI Index: AMR 28/014/2000).

41 *El Universo,* "Sidosos en la Primero de Mayo", 5 July 2000; *Expreso de Guayaquil,* "Gays con SIDA andan sueltos", 5 July 2000.

42 *UNAIDS Policy on HIV testing and counselling,* UN Doc. UNAIDS/97.2, August 1997.

43 *Venezuela: Fear for the safety of the transgendered community in Valencia, Carabobo State* (AI Index: AMR 53/009/2000).

44 *Argentina: AI Communication to Minister of Interior, December 1997* (AI Index: AMR 13/016/1997).

45 *Argentina: Vanessa Piedrabuena — Fear for Safety* (AI Index: AMR 13/011/2000).

46 *Transvestites condemned to sex trade to survive,* IPS, 3 October 2000.

47 Stonewall Day commemorates protests that took place in New York City, USA, in 1969 in which the local LGBT community took to the streets to demonstrate against police raids, harassment and ill-treatment. Stonewall is the name of the bar that was raided on 28 June 1969, precipitating the protests.

48 Not his real name.

49 Statement by "Tomás", name withheld, to the *Comite Permanente por la Defensa de los Derechos Humanos.*

50 *Comite Permanente por la Defensa de los Derechos Humanos.*

51 *Human Rights Violations against Sexual Minorities in India, A PUCL-K Fact-finding Report about Bangalore,* People's Union for Civil Liberties-Karnataka, February 2001.

52 Alan Elsner, "Rampant rape in US prisons traumatizes victims;" Reuters, 17 January 2001.

53 *Mexico: Death threats/fear for safety* (AI Index: AMR 41/064/2000) and *Mexico: Further information on death threats/fear for safety* (AI Index: 41/003/2001).

54 *Jamaica: A Summary of Concerns: A Briefing for the Human Rights Committee* (AMR 38/007/1997).

55 Tom Cahill, from "Stop Prisoner Rape, Inc.", as reported in Elsner, "Rampant rape in US prisons traumatizes victims;" Reuters, 17 January 2001.

56 Cahill, ibid.

57 *United States of America: Californian Prisons: Failure to protect prisoners from abuse — Amnesty International's continuing concerns* (AI Index: AMR 51/079/2000).

58 *United States of America: Violations in West Virginia Jails* (AI Index: AMR 51/109/2000)

59 *All Too Familiar: Sexual Abuse of Women in U.S. State Prisons*, Human Rights Watch Women's Rights Project, 1996.

60 *USA: Rights for All "Not Part of My Sentence" — Violations of the human rights of women in custody* (AI Index: AMR 51/001/1999).

61 "Trois surveillants de la prison de Fleury-Mérogis condamnés pour agressions sexuelles sur des travestis", *Le Monde*, 2 February 1999.

62 "Trois gardiens abusaient des travestis", *Le Parisien*, 2 February 1999.

63 Report of the Committee for the Prevention of Torture and Inhuman or Degrading Treatment or Punishment following its visit to France, 6-18 October 1996, CPT/Inf (98) 7, 14 May 1998, pp 36 and 79.

64 *Le Monde*, "Six surveillants de Fleury déférés pour avoir abusé de travestis détenus", 18 October 1996.

65 "A Fleury, marché sexuel entre gardiens et travestis", *Libération*, 16 October 1996.

66 "Trois surveillants de la prison de Fleury-Mérogis condamnés pour agressions sexuelles sur des travestis", *Le Monde*, 2 February 1999.

67 *The Rights of Lesbians and Gay Men in the Russian Federation*, An International Gay and Lesbian Human Rights Commission report by Masha Gessen.

68 *Pitcherskaia v. INS*, 118 F.3d 641 (9th Cir. 1997), 24 June 1997. As of September 2000, this case was still pending in the Board of Immigration Appeals. See also Shannon Minter, in "Unspoken Rules: Sexual Orientation and Women's Human Rights;" International Gay and Lesbian Human Rights Commission, 1995, pp. 222, 223.

69 *The Aversion Project: Human rights abuses of gays and lesbians in the SADF by health workers during the apartheid era*, Mikki van Zyl, Jeanelle de Gruchy, Sheila Lapinsky, Simon Lewin, and Graeme Reid, Simply Said and Done, Cape Town, October 1999.

70 National Coalition of Gay and Lesbian Equality, Request for the Appointment of a Commission of Inquiry, August 14, 2000. Letter addressed to Honourable Minister of Defence, Mosiuoa Patrick Gerard Lekota, MP.

71 *An Ambulance of the Wrong Colour: Health Professionals, Human Rights and Ethics in South Africa*, Laurel Baldwin-Ragaven, Jeanelle de Gruchy and Leslie London, University of Cape Town,1999.

72 World Health Organization, International Statistical Classification of Diseases and Related Health Problems, 10th revision (ICD 10), Geneva, 1992.

73 Chinese Psychiatric Association, March 2001.

74 The quotation was cited in an interview in December 1994 by Bev Clark, author of *Lesbian Activism in Zimbabwe*.

75 UN Doc. E/CN.4/1996/53, para. 32.

76 *Velasquez-Rodriguez*, (ser. C) No. 4, Judgment of 29 July 1988, para. 172.

77 Ibid., para. 174.

78 Case of *A v. the United Kingdom* (application 25599/94), Judgment of 23 September 1988.

79 President Robert Mugabe at the opening of the Zimbabwe International Bookfair on Human Rights and Justice, August 1995.

80 Not her real name.

81 Lesbian and Gay Immigration Rights Task Force, New York, USA: interview with Irina, February 2000. Irina's claim was denied because of a procedural technicality.

82 "Sri Lanka's Press Council Attacks Lesbianism", *BBC Online News*, June 2, 2000.

83 Report of the Special Rapporteur on violence against women, its causes and consequences, Commission on Human Rights, UN Doc. E/CN.4/1997/47, 12 February 1997.

84 See, for example, "Violence Against Lesbians", Shirley Lesser, pp. 42-46 (Part 2 of 2), Vol. 13, *A Journal About Women*, Iris, 1993 and *Hidden from History: Reclaiming the Gay and Lesbian Past*, Martin Duberman, Martha Vicinus and George Chauncey Jr, eds, New York: Penguin, 1989.

85 Lambda Legal Defense Fund, New York, USA, interview with Derek Henkle; www.lambdalegal.org

86 Lesbian and Gay Immigration Rights Task Force, New York, USA, Status Report 2000, No. 1.

87 *Gay-Hate Related Homicides: An overview of major findings in New South Wales*, Australian Institute of Criminology, June 2000.

88 UNHCR, *Protecting Refugees: Questions and Answers*, UNHCR/PI/Q&A-UK1.PM/Feb.1996, at 12.

89 International Lesbian and Gay Association.

90 *United States of America: Lost in the labyrinth — the detention of asylum-seekers* (AI Index: AMR 51/115/1999).

91 This quotation was cited in October 1997 at a New York University Law School panel presentation by Saeed Rahman, author of "Shifting Grounds for Asylum: Female Genital Surgery and Sexual Orientation", *Columbia Human Rights Law Review*, 29:2: 467, p. 516.

92 Letter to United States Department of Justice, Office of the Inspector General; Catholic Legal Immigration Network Inc, August 4, 1999.

93 Refugee Status Appeal Authority, Refugee Appeal No. 1312/93 (Re GJ), Aug 30/95.

94 Juris Lavrikovs, 22 July 1998, as cited in the ILGA World Legal Survey — *Latvia/Asylum entry*, www.ilga.org/Information/legal_survey/Europe/latvia.htm

95 "Gays seek Political Asylum in SA" www.q.co.za/news/1999/9911/991108-gayasylum.htm

96 *Hernandez-Montiel v. Immigration and Naturalization Services*, F.3d, No. 98-70582 (9th Cir. 24 August 2000).

97 *Human Rights Violations against Sexual Minorities in India*, A PUCL-K Fact-finding Report about Bangalore, People's Union for Civil Liberties-Karnataka, February 2001.

98 "Zambian gays and lesbians in impasse", *Gay and Lesbian Times*, 10 February 2001.

99 Report of the Special Representative of the UN Secretary-General on human rights defenders to the Commission on Human Rights, March 2001, UN Doc. E/CN.4/2001/94, para 89, part VII.

100 See for example, the 1975 Declaration of Tokyo by the World Medical Association which enjoins doctors not to participate in torture "whatever the victim's beliefs" and underlines that the doctor's role is to "alleviate suffering" of his or her patients.

101 For instance, Article 2 of the ICCPR obliges states parties to take all reasonable steps to protect all rights without discrimination. Article 17 prohibits "unlawful attacks" on any person's "honour and reputation", and obliges states parties to provide protection, through the law, against such attacks.

102 Executive committee of the UN High Commissioner for Refugees (EXCOM), conclusion 44.

WHAT YOU CAN DO

- Join our campaign — **Take a step to stamp out torture.**
  You can help stamp out torture. Add your voice to Amnesty International's campaign. Help us to make a difference. Contact your national office of Amnesty International and ask for information about how to join the campaign, including information on how to take action on some of the specific cases featured in this report.
- Become a member of Amnesty International and other local and international human rights organizations which fight torture.
- Make a donation to support Amnesty International's work.
- Tell friends and family about the campaign and ask them to join too.

Campaigning Online

The website **www.stoptorture.org** allows visitors to access Amnesty International's information about torture. It will also offer the opportunity to appeal on behalf of individuals at risk of being tortured. Those registering onto the site will receive urgent e-mail messages alerting them to take action during the campaign.

- Register to take action against torture at **www.stoptorture.org**

☐ I would like to join your campaign. Please send me more information.
☐ I would like to join Amnesty International. Please send me details.
☐ I would like to donate to Amnesty International's campaign to stamp out torture.

Credit card number: ☐☐☐☐ ☐☐☐☐ ☐☐☐☐ ☐☐☐☐

Expiry date   /   £   [amount]

Signature

Name

Address

Please photocopy this coupon and send it to:
Amnesty International, International Secretariat, Campaign against Torture,
1 Easton Street, London WC1X 0DW, United Kingdom